"*Engaging Leadership* succeeds in demonstrating the critical importance for leaders to work on three motivational fronts at the same time: they must be intellectually clear and convincing, their acts must support and exemplify the strategic intent, and they must be able to create the conditions for success by building a strong emotional agenda."
Arthur Yeung, Associate Dean and Philips Chair Professor of HRM, CEIBS, Ex-CHO, Acer Group

"Short, to the point, and politically incorrect, this book is also very deep and well documented. *Engaging Leadership* is the best recipe book on how to encourage large numbers of people into a new direction."
Michel Abitbol, CEO, Elle et Lui Group

"This book, based on years of experience with executives from many companies and industries, provides us with valuable practical insight on how to change our own and others' behavior in order to accelerate implementation and develop new skills, and on the value of strategy. It succeeds in addressing burning issues for practicing managers."
Juan Rada, Senior Vice President, Public Sector and Education Business Unit, Oracle Corporation Europe

ENGAGING LEADERSHIP

Three Agendas for Sustaining Achievement

Didier Marlier,

Chris Parker

and

Mobilizing Teams International

palgrave
macmillan

First published 2009 by
PALGRAVE MACMILLAN

Palgrave Macmillan in the UK is an imprint of Macmillan Publishers Limited, registered in England, company number 785998, of Houndmills, Basingstoke, Hampshire RG21 6XS.

Palgrave Macmillan in the US is a division of St Martin's Press LLC, 175 Fifth Avenue, New York, NY 10010.

Palgrave Macmillan is the global academic imprint of the above companies and has companies and representatives throughout the world.

Palgrave® and Macmillan® are registered trademarks in the United States, the United Kingdom, Europe and other countries

ISBN-13: 978-0-230-57752-7
ISBN-10: 0-230-57752-0

This book is printed on paper suitable for recycling and made from fully managed and sustained forest sources. Logging, pulping and manufacturing processes are expected to conform to the environmental regulations of the country of origin.

A catalogue record for this book is available from the British Library.

A catalog record for this book is available from the Library of Congress.

10 9 8 7 6 5 4 3 2 1
18 17 16 15 14 13 12 11 10 09

Printed and bound in Great Britain by
CPI Antony Rowe, Chippenham and Eastbourne

CONTENTS

FIGURES

HOW THIS BOOK WAS CONCEIVED

Chris and Didier met in IMD in 1988, as professor and student.[1] For Didier, Chris was an unorthodox, lively, passionate, and generous leadership professor. For Chris, Didier was a rebellious, pony-tailed MBA student with a high potential.

Eight years later they met again in a bar in Lutry (Switzerland), sharing the same frustration that both the academic institutions and the strategy consultancies were failing to support their clients in terms of real behavioral change.

They therefore decided to respond to the "Call for adventure" (see Chapter 6) and engage in their "heroic journey," Chris leaving a well-paid, highly regarded tenure at IMD, Didier burying his dream of becoming a partner with the consulting firm he was working for.

An informal gathering in 2003 in Villars of 20 consultants and academics gave birth to the MTI Network with which they are fully engaged today.[2]

This network is resolutely pragmatic, hands-on and down to earth in its approach, as we hope this book will also be. We have not attempted to write an academic thesis or essay; we have gathered and summarized our experience in leadership engagement and tried to share it with you.

Together, we are moved by a set of evolving beliefs. Here is where these are today:

- Clarity, meaning, and capacity to influence are crucial if an organization intends to engage its employees in changes which produce long-lasting results.
- Reality is constructed by the language we use: The recurring language people hear in organizations is what will focus their attention.
- "People are more likely to act their way into a new way of thinking

than think their way into a new way of acting."[3] Behavioral change takes place through feedback and experimentation with new value-creating behaviors rather than through preaching and slide shows. Just try it and build from there.

- Stories and behaviors are more powerful than strategies. People believe in what they see. Strategy becomes an illusion if leaders do not consistently walk the talk. People retain stories more than facts.

- Engage rather than selling: Engaging leaders mobilize their teams' intellectual, emotional, and creative capacities, rather than trying to sell change to a passive audience. People desire engagement!

- Exploration and conclusion: Leaders who explore with their teams prior to driving conclusions create a unique competitive advantage for their organizations. Engage then plan as much as plan and engage!

- Working on the three agendas: The basis for sustainable business success rests upon co-creating clarity around the strategic agenda (*logos*), defining the rules of engagement which will support it (*ethos*), and setting conditions for people to do and be their best (*pathos*). People engage when there is coherence between the three agendas.

- Recovery from setbacks is a skill set that can be learned. "Being on the edge" or "ahead of the pack" is a creative state where people make mistakes. Courageous vulnerability is an engaging quality.

THE AUTHORS

Chris Parker (British, BA, MA, C. Psychology, chartered occupational psychologist) has been teaching organizational behavior and leadership at Cranfield (Director of In-Company Programs 1979-86) and IMD (professor 1986-96). The purpose underlying all Chris's professional work is to help leaders create the conditions for themselves and others to be and do their best. He is driven by releasing potential and energy, and working with the positive human core.

Email: chris@mobilizinteams.com
tel: +4121795002

Didier Marlier (Belgian/Swiss, BA in law and MBA, IMD) has lost the pony tail of his IMD days but not his capacity to challenge purposefully. He has been a strategy consultant and taught change and leadership as an associate professor at Nyenrode and visiting faculty member at INSEAD and EHL. Didier's professional goal is to make the workplace an energizing environment so that people may perform at their best. He is driven by authenticity, competence, and generosity.

Email: Didier@enablersnetwork.com/didier@mobilizingteams.com/
tel: +41 794351660

The partners who have contributed to this book are:

Email:
Bob@transformationstrategies.com /
bob@mobilizingteams.com
tel: + 1 301.887-0220

Bob Devlin is a senior level consultant, facilitator and coach. He is also president of Transformation Strategies, Inc. Bob is an American citizen who has lived and travelled internationally most of his life—growing up in Belgium and living in East Africa for four years as a Peace Corps volunteer and trainer in the early 1980s. He is a student of Yoga and Chinese Philosophy and incorporates the Sedona Method in his work.

Email:
philippe@mobilizingteams.com
tel: +41 79 4135906

Swiss born, Philippe Graf holds a Master in Psychology of Intervention from the Valence University (Spain) and a BA in Hotel Management from EHL. He has been studying and practicing Martial Arts since 1968. After starting with Judo, he then went to Jui-Jitsu, Karate and Aïkido. A professor for ten years, he started to study the relationship between energy and movement in Aïkido, which led him to the discovery of Seitaï, an area he has been deepening since 1986. Setaï can best be described as a blend of ancestral oriental wisdom updated with the most recent findings in neurology and anatomy.

Email:
nmcroberts@keymove.fr /
nick@mobilizingteams.com
tel: +33 6 78712072

Nicholas McRoberts is Australian and French. He came to leadership engagement processes through study in both classical music (conducting) and information technology and relational systems. Constantly advancing both sides of his professional agenda, Nick is regularly invited to participate in international conducting master-classes all over Europe (Spain, Italy, Norway) while maintaining a busy consulting agenda. Based in Paris, today Nick shares his time between France and Australia.

Claire Meany is a senior level consultant, facilitator, coach and Vice President of Transformation Strategies, Inc. Claire is an American citizen who has lived in New York, Washington, DC and California. She has travelled extensively in the United States and abroad and enjoys experiencing different cultures. She is a student of Martial Arts and holds the rank of Second Degree black belt and training instructor in Tae Kwon Do.

Email:
Claire@transformationstrategies.com /
Claire@mobilizingteams.com
tel: + 1 301.887-0220

Email:
tritia.neeb@djihn.nl/
tritia@mobilzingteams.com
tel: +31 613-880-944

Tritia Neeb (Dutch, Masters in Social Science and BBA) has been a project and line manager in IT for 12 years. She now works as a team coach. Tritia's professional purpose is to enable people and teams to use their strengths to "make a difference." She is driven by passion, curiosity, and a deep respect for living beings.

Email:
Newman2 Michael@aol.com/
michael@mobilizingteams.com
tel: +44 1606 881699

Michael Newman (British, MSc in GIS) has been an international leadership consultant for ten years. In this capacity he can apply tough lessons he learnt in manufacturing, mountaineering, and as an army officer. His goal is to see value created by the application of skillful leadership in business. He is driven by the desire for continuous learning and for freedom to choose how to apply his expertise.

Email:
stephen@nowconsulting.co.uk/
stephen@mobilizingteams.com/
tel: +44 7879485957

Stephen Okunowo holds a BA (Honours) and PGCE and developed his interest in the impact of the behavioural and emotional agenda on performance during his time as a survival specialist and then as a disaster manager where the ability to lead a team and deliver exemplary results during extreme uncertainty were critical success criteria.

Email:
tony@pageconsulting.co.uk/
tony@mobilizingteams.com/
tel: +44 797-123-9529

Tony Page (British, chartered psychologist) is a leadership consultant who strives to bring executives and teams into close understanding of their "real work," particularly during periods of significant upheaval. He aligns board members and top teams with each other and with the senior leadership community across an enterprise. A prominent practitioner in the field of leadership and change, Tony is also the well-known author of two groundbreaking books: *Diary of a Change Agent* (1996) and *From Hippos to Gazelles: How leaders create leaders* (2008).

Email:
Ben@mobilizingteams.com
tel: +41 78 7175086

Ben Parker (British/Swiss, BSc course in international hospitality management and MSc in the psychology of work) has been working in leadership consulting since 2004. Ben focuses on getting people to engage with their intentions, to fully grasp their potential and release it in ways that create sustainable performance. He values people who tap into their true selves and then use this with their colleagues and subordinates to create an environment of honesty and trust.

Alex Villar Hauser (Austrian/Spanish/ British, BA, counseling psychologist) has been working as a change leader and a coach to senior leaders since 1993. Alex now works in facilitating and consulting in multi-organizational partnerships, specializing in mergers and acquisitions and large-scale organizational change. Alex's fundamental professional purpose is to facilitate high-quality conversations to measurably improve performance and value creation in complex and multi-dimensional contexts.

Email:
Jarron20@aol.com /
alex@mobilizingteams.com
tel: +44 7768 143 644

Email:
Nick.VanHeck@elpnetwork.com
tel: +32 16 24 19 10

Nick van Heck (Belgian) advises organizations and their leaders on designing and implementing strategy engagement processes. Nick is a former research and teaching assistant, and visiting faculty member at a variety of business schools around Europe (Solvay Business School, the Catholic University of Leuven, INSEAD, and others), and author of a management book on the leadership challenges in globalizing organizations. He created with colleagues the "Executive Learning Partnership," based on his deeply held beliefs around "(re-)insourcing the strategic and leadership thinking and acting into the organization" and "reaching for leaders' heads, hearts, and hands."

ACKNOWLEDGMENTS

Cris, obrigado para ser essa pessoa maravilhosa, a imagem do Amor Incondicional. Te devo tudo!

Betinho, obrigado para tua integridade e honestidade. Gosto de te ver resolvido a seguir teu sonho musical. Estou orgulhoso de voce!

Marcos, obrigado para ser um filho cheio de Amor e Compaixão apesar de tudo que voce teve que encarar na sua vida. Confio no seu futuro!

Thaïs, obrigado para ser o Anjo que guarda sua familia. Obrigado para ser uma pessoa de tanta responsabilidade e amor, ja na sua idade. Te admiro!

Henri Plomb, Patrice Méan, Gérard Dienne, Jose-Carlos Ribeiro, and ... Chris Parker, thank you for having replaced the guidance and affection of a father gone too early.

Didier (Summer 2008)

Thanks to my wife Maureen for everyday deep emotional support; thanks to Ben and Dan for keeping me grounded in human reality. Thanks to all the network members for their challenge and support. Thanks to Didier for driving this book project, and thanks to all our clients who keep inviting us to do exciting things

Chris (Summer 2008)

PURPOSE AND STRUCTURE

People don't follow strategies, they follow behaviors!

Stories are more powerful than strategies!

Chris is purposefully provocative when he addresses large audiences of executives in public speeches and in-company seminars. He emphasizes that the power of "strategy" has been overdone in the recent business history. Behaviors, passion, and energy are the "Holy Grail" we should be looking for, not the illusory "right strategy."

In today's internet-speed environment, passionate commitment to being ahead of the game is as important as having the right strategy. In Toyota, senior managers preach: "Reform business when business is good." They demand the apparently impossible and, while there is a definite hierarchy, they insist that people argue for new approaches, and provide training and tools to do that in a "professional way." They break classic rules of strategy, trying to do too much. They put customers first, dealers second, and the company last.[1] Their passionate culture gives them the competitive advantage that many seek to emulate. Their customers keep on buying repeatedly and the company has so much cash that it is referred to as Toyota Bank by many today.

In the summer of 2007, we were listening to a conversation among leaders of a team that was pivotal to the success of a large merger between two European companies. They were commenting the recent visit to their office by the CEO. The feedback was:

"He was cold and distant, and his presentation was so polished that it came across as unauthentic."

"What was he really trying to say?"

"Can we believe him?"

"Was he sincere when complimenting our team?"

"His vision was vague and unclear to me."

"He came across as disengaged and consequently disengaged me."

"He had no convincing story about the merger."

"I am worried; he doesn't seem to understand our company's culture or value it."

To make things worse, the team leader had just come back from a top management meeting that was intended to create a company-wide engagement process. This process was driven by a very well-known and well-intentioned strategy consulting firm. The consultants' focus on strategy was evident but it was only a consolidation of what everyone expected. There was nothing engaging, let alone inspiring. The best one could say was that enthusiasm wasn't sky-high: "Basically, we didn't learn anything new. ... It was a rather flat non-event. ... It was process driven. ... The mistrust between the merging partners hasn't gone away. ... There is a lack of clarity. ... A lot of people are disillusioned. ... Our colleagues were disappointed by the new style of working. ... We should keep up our old culture and strengthen our solidarity—there are tough times ahead."

Why on earth, we were thinking, did the consultants move away from their field of expertise (selling ideas and presentations) to a place where their lack of real ability was so blatantly obvious (engagement and implementation)?

Engaging Leadership is our contribution to the huge transformations that businesses need to achieve if they wish to survive in tomorrow's ever-faster changing environment. Many boards, management teams, and individual leaders voice their convictions: maintaining the organizational status quo when everything moves so rapidly around us makes no logical sense; change is essential—but in which direction and how? This book is the summary of our collective experience in guiding change. The intention is to demystify and not theorize. It is not a "21-step recipe" book; it is about how "everyday leaders" can guide people through more gratifying journeys towards success.

THE STRUCTURE

We have attempted to keep this book as short and meaningful as possible. Like us, you may be sick and tired of those "management books" where the real content could have been summarized in five pages, but for some reason has been diluted into a 450-page brick instead.

Here is how the book is structured:

- Chapter 1 builds the case for the change that is needed in the way we lead our organizations. It provides an overview of the "three agendas of leadership."
- Chapter 2 clarifies what we mean by the "strategic/intellectual agenda" and suggests ways to engage people in it.
- Chapter 3 looks at how leaders should lead through value-building behaviors, and the consequences of not doing so.
- Chapter 4 studies the "emotional agenda." It attempts to demonstrate that this is a vital, bottom-line-oriented element of successfully leading towards sustainable results.
- Chapter 5 ties all this together; it offers a robust three-step process to lead people through change and explains what the leadership engagement process is about.
- Chapter 6 draws a parallel between Joseph Campbell's celebrated research on the universal myth (termed the Monomyth) and the journey of leaders on their way to success.

CHAPTER 1

THE NEED FOR A NEW
LEADERSHIP STYLE

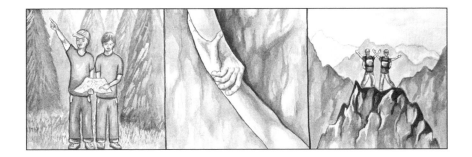

FROM THE CERTAINTY OF THE *TRENTE GLORIEUSES* TO THE AMBIGUITIES OF "OPEN SOURCE LEADERSHIP"

From Jean-Christophe Rufin's *Empire and the New Barbarians* or Alvin Toffler's *Third Wave*, to Peter Senge's *Fifth Discipline* or Joe Javorski's *Synchronicity*, many authors have shared their intuitions that a tsunami was about to transform the geopolitical, economic, social, and leadership world in which we live.[1]

Many have attempted in all sorts of ways to explain why this is happening, from George W. Bush's simplistic "axis of evil" to Friedman's sophisticated "ten forces that flattened the world."[2]

In our view, there is a historical trend that is moving leaders from the traditional, experience-based, and paternalistic style towards what a Nokia executive calls "open source leadership."

The *Trente Glorieuses*

From a historical perspective, one can say that the post-war years (1945–75), usually referred to in France as the "Thirty Glorious," were times when there was no need for great consultants; shattered societies and infrastructures had to be rebuilt across vast swathes of Europe, Japan, and many other parts of the world. Almost anything people might undertake was sure to be an improvement on the past and would create value for individuals and their communities. The leadership style was paternalistic and experience based: "I lead and deserve respect because of my experience!" Organizations were largely pyramidal, based on Taylor's work philosophy,[3] hierarchy was rigid, seniority meant superiority—no questions allowed, no challenges welcome, just do your work and what you are paid for. When Didier was at university, one famous professor started his first lecture by declaring in front of 500 students: "You will sit here for one year. There will only be three acceptable behaviors: listening, taking notes, and remaining silent. My starting assumption is that you are all ignorant, so no comments or questions would be of any value to the rest of the audience." And after this promising introduction they went through a whole year in monastic silence while the ex-banker shared his wisdom.

The leadership style in the "30 glorious years" was closest to the "buffalo style of leadership" that Belasco and Stayer describe in their book *Flight of the Buffalo* (see also the excellent article Stayer wrote for the *Harvard Business Review*, "How I learned to let my workers lead").[4]

The "MBA years"

Then came the period from the 1980s to the 2000s, labeled the "MBA years."[5] A change of focus was triggered by feedback from recruiters who complained to the then MBA Director of IMD, Kamran Kashani that "business school students were excellent performers ... as long as they were told what to do and how to do it," but that they were hopeless under fast-changing business conditions. They feared ambiguity. These were the golden years of financial analysts, strategy consultants, quantitative analysis, and the like. We entered an era of scientific leadership when predictions, forecasts, and striving for certainty were the rule. Strategies became increasingly important: niche markets, globalization—everything was coalescing to fine tune and to specify the context while maintaining stability around content. Organizations became increasingly complex, corporate functions of all types grew like mushrooms, the need for centralized knowledge and leadership was paramount. Within matrix organizations, more and more structure appeared. Leadership was based on knowledge, which became the source of power. Companies were living under the aegis of strategic planning, and we, as business school students, were dragged through useless class sessions about regression-analysis-based decision making.[6] Leadership was based on knowledge. Knowledge was the basis of everything and "content leadership" was the license to operate without which leaders had no credibility. "Bright" people got the leadership jobs, people with big brains but little empathy and a distant manner.

In our experience of working with hundreds of active leaders each year, many of them still operate with the implicit belief that this is the context in which they exist and that they should therefore be strong "content" leaders—that they are leaders because they "know more" than the others.

One senior banker we worked with recognized this flaw in his thinking when he was given the job of directing a group of "Linux Wizards" who were producing very dynamic hedge fund management algorithms. It was impossible for him to understand what they were doing or how it related to what his other fund managers did, but they were producing amazing results. On top of that they wore sandals and came to work on bicycles; one even brought his dog to the office in Threadneedle Street! The banker's process of adjustment was painful but short: Admit you are vulnerable, listen intently to proposed outcomes, and create the right conditions. We knew he had changed when he said "My dear chap I know f... all about Linux and Fortran, but I know now what nerds need in order to be successful!"

The paradigm shift

In the early 1990s the first cracks in the wall appeared, literally and figuratively. In geopolitics we saw the end of the Berlin Wall, and many of the things that had been held up as truths needed to be re-assessed. The Pentagon's strategists had to find a new preferred enemy to confront since the Communist regime had clearly imploded. And on the business front, interesting elements started to emerge. The spring of 1996 saw one of the biggest falls in Wall Street's history.[7] Analysts quoted by the Swiss financial daily *L'AGEFI* explained it thus: "Everything is under control: We've never had so many new house starts, never sold so many new cars, and never had such low unemployment levels. This all means inflationary pressures, which in turn implies that the Federal Reserve could hike up rates and guess what? The stock exchange didn't like it!" Fine! The problem is that six months later there was the biggest rise in share prices that Wall Street had ever seen. How do you think analysts explained it? Now, please *do not look* at the next page. Guess first.

Did you guess? Financial analysts explained that complete U-turn in the market by citing *exactly the same factors*, giving them a positive twist this time: "This all means that the US economy is booming and Wall Street likes it." In other words, they tried to explain new situations with old rules. Nobody today would reject the argument that the Dow Jones is as much driven by emotion as rationality. And in late 2008 when panic seems to have replaced fundamentals, it is interesting to see how many articles proclaim that fear has taken over from logic. After Aids, SARS, bird flu, and oil prices, here comes a new terror wave: financial crisis.

The psychologist Daniel Kahneman received the Nobel Prize in 2002 for his work on the irrational and idiosyncratic in behavioral economics and stock markets. This is all part of what we see as the paradigm shift of the 1990s. Albert Einstein's famous remark still rings very true: "We can't solve problems by using the same kind of thinking we used when we created them." The geopolitical changes of the early 1990s brought uncertainties, paradoxes, and ambiguity into the game. Those hoping for a predictable world started to feel uncomfortable. "You know, when we did our MBA, they surely taught us wonderful things about strategy, discounted cash flows, and probabilities helping the decision-making process, but no one told us how to deal with the local mafia, which is what I am confronted with in my new job in Moscow," confided a disappointed MBA graduate, as early as 1992.

The intersection between competition and cooperation was summed up in a neologism: coopetition. What are LG, HTC, Sony-Erickson, or Samsung to Nokia mobile phones? Competitors? Certainly, in the narrowest definition of the handset battlefield. But how are we to define Microsoft or Google then, in relation to the mobile phone industry? And what about iPhone, Google-HTC or Skype and other VOIPs? All sides are competing in the race for internet enablement. Nokia is licensing its software to its otherwise close competitors, in the hope of making it the norm for that new industry. Microsoft ignored Linux for so long, then suddenly signs of solid interest were reported in the press in late 2006.

What could potentially be a huge threat to credit/debit cards? The mobile phone industry, with the technology of bar-code readers coupled to handsets. And what could be the threat to mobile phones? Research undertaken in the area of brain and telepathy maybe? Or more simply Google's claim that the future of connectivity will be in a "smart network" that will enable mobile devices to become smarter? Those of us familiar with mergers and takeover stories will remember the stunningly hostile reaction of the world's leading banks in 1995 to the apparently insignificant move by Microsoft to purchase Intuit, a successful maker of software for the banking sector. They had immediately understood that the move, if successful, could make Microsoft extremely dangerous for them, linking its software with online banking capacities.

This paradigm shift has also had a profound impact on leadership styles and the way we organize ourselves. If, in earlier years, leaders were expected to know (by experience and/or seniority), this became a very risky bet in the 2000s. How can leaders pretend to lead by knowledge when the knowledge is changing at so fast a pace? They need to move towards a more engaging, involving style of leadership. Shaping the context rather than leading the content becomes *the* challenge for leaders who previously built their credibility on being content experts. This is a fundamental change for many leaders, whatever level they operate at, in business, politics, and sport. Leaders have to start learning to become less isolated and more team players, just like Belasco and Stayer's wild geese. This leadership style is new to many; mistakes have to be experienced and admitted and experiments allowed. We have called this "transition leadership."

Open source leadership: Reasons for hope or despair?

So what is next? Don Tapscott and Anthony Williams in their book *Wikinomics* argue that the internet is having a profound effect on business and business culture.[8] They claim that the internet is an entirely different environment from the one in which we currently operate and is characterized by three fundamentals: it is flat, it is connected, and it is democratic. It is these elements that have enabled the whole "open source" concept to emerge, with people collaborating and working together in totally different ways from before. The open source phenomenon has now accelerated to a level where it is clear it will have a huge impact on the way companies and organizations work and innovate in the future.

How do we recognize such an environment? Goals and objectives may not be what they seemed. What was clear and agreed upon yesterday is suddenly different today. Reorganizations follow restructurings which preceded the "new vision," "new strategy"... How can we respond to such permanently moving targets? Yesterday's winning formulas don't seem to work any more and a lot of experimentation is needed. It would be foolishness to try to respond with old reflexes to a totally new type of situation. We are witnessing the transition from organizations to organisms.

When describing this historical perspective to participants at our seminars, we usually get a strong reaction:

> We recognize this era of "open source leadership." The problem is that our leaders/we continue to act and lead with the assumptions and style of the "MBA years." When something goes wrong, the reply is "Call in the consultants, reorganize the org. chart, get a new strategy..." They/we don't try to challenge our own mindsets first!

And how accurate those comments are!

Nokia's leaders challenged that mindset in 2007, when they decided to radically challenge their ways of thinking and organizing (when the company was at the top of its industry, having a larger market share than its three closest competitors combined). How many other instances do we know where leaders have chosen to address the symptoms instead of the cause? How many of us have the courage to go back to the "causal drawing board" and address the issues of leadership and engagement? For some it seems easier to tackle that critical problem by creating a "Leadership Department" that will bear the responsibility and blame, as a US investment bank is reported to have done a few years ago.

How does one lead in the open source era? This is precisely the theme of this book, *Engaging Leadership*. In short, engaging leaders focus their energy on the process/context of leading as much as the content. They consider themselves in charge of raising issues and running the problem-solving process, rather than trying to solve the problems by themselves.

They understand that leadership is about fulfilling their followers' expectations around the intellectual agenda, by providing them with a coherent logic of why things should change, displaying behaviors in line with the new strategic intent, and creating the conditions for their people to do and be their best. Recent studies by Barbara Fredrickson and Marcial Losada of high-performing business teams have found that "it's the context, stupid."[9] Flourishing business groups have an external rather than an internal focus; they have more positive communication than negative (five acts to one); they ask empathic questions of each other, meaning they are clearly interested in the response; they balance advocacy with enquiry; and they build more connections inside the team than average teams (twice as many) or poorly performing ones (three times as many). Losada was able to predict the performance of teams by observing their micro-behaviors with no content analysis of the communication!

There is a profound change taking place in the business world. The leadership culture has evolved from the paternalistic, authoritarian style to the content, expert-leadership assumption, and will be rapidly progressing towards open source leadership.

What else is changing in the competitive environment?

THE VALUE MATRIX: A CHALLENGE TO WALL-STREET-DRIVEN STRATEGIES

Our colleagues Paul Verdin and Nick van Heck (INSEAD, Solvay, and ELP) have made a large-scale statistical analysis of what made companies sustainably successful.[10] After a lot of number crunching they

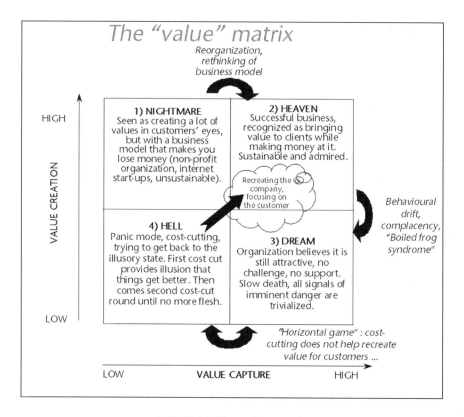

FIGURE 1.1 **The value matrix**

realized that success was independent of competition, home markets, or economic conditions. The most important criterion in explaining a company's success was the company itself, its focus on customers and the what, how, and where of delivery. They pulled this work together in the "value matrix."

On the vertical axis is "value creation" (high/low). This is the value brought by a firm, a product, or a service, as perceived by the customers. On the horizontal axis is "value capture," meaning the value that the firm is creating for itself (the bottom line), which can in turn be high or low.

The nightmare

A start-up company will kick off with a great idea, new service, or revolutionary product or technology. Unfortunately, as many dot-com investors learned when they got their fingers burnt, a great idea doesn't guarantee financial viability. How many years did it take for Amazon to finally create financial value for its shareholders? What is the business model of Skype? Why did eBay purchase it? What is the financial sustainability of YouTube and what did Google have in mind when taking it over? And these are success stories—or at least celebrated as such by Wall Street—and for a few successes, how many failures? The nightmare box is about having a great idea which will rapidly attract customers but is not supported (yet) by a money-making business model. The leadership culture here is typical of start-up: hype, passion, swimming pool in the middle of the garden, Bermuda shorts, and creativity. Which of us hasn't dreamt of working in such an inspiring environment?

Heaven

However, as we all know, fairy tales have an end. It is estimated that only 10 percent of small businesses survive their first five years of existence. That certainly differs between continents but the principle probably remains valid: many businesses die young, even though they are based on good ideas. To be sustainable, businesses usually need to grow from their adolescence to something more mature. We are now moving towards "Heaven," where companies still provide great value to their customers whilst, having redesigned their business model, they also cash in on that success. In cultural terms, we go for less "fun and inspirational times": finance people become stronger, a bit of seriousness is brought in, processes, procedures, measurement, and reporting make their appearance. Ideas are properly weighed, some are dropped and some are kept. The business is taking off and some of the most disturbing and rebellious minds take off too—towards another destination. Remember Steve Jobs leaving Apple a long time ago, to be replaced by John Sculley and a team of serious professional managers?

The company finally becomes a "Wall Street darling." The CEO is all over *Fortune Magazine* and *Forbes*, and the guru-addicted fans have their new hero.

The dream

Sadly, the law of gravity applies to even the best businesses. Organizations drift towards the world of "dream." Peter Senge calls this the "boiled frog syndrome": throw a living frog into hot water and it will instantly jump out. Throw it into cold water and turn the heat up little by little, and the frog will die, boiled and happy (and here comes a lawsuit against us for sharing a recipe on how to be cruel to animals). This applies to business; it is called complacency, arrogance, market dominance. The biggest threat to the Googles, eBays, Microsofts, or Nokias of this world comes when they rigidify into "serious businesses." When talking to friends in such prestigious companies, we find their worries are strikingly similar: "Where have the passion, craziness, and boldness gone? We are in danger of becoming procedure driven, CFO oriented; the only department which grows steadily is the Business Controllers'. We hire PhDs and MBAs but turn down those wild, maverick trouble-makers who created the company's reputation and wrote its history ..."

Very often, the culture becomes "Don't challenge the leaders." Seniority means superiority; the cultural orthodoxy is not to be challenged—"Love it or leave it" as Brazilian military dictators used to retort in the 1970s when confronted by (rare) courageous critics. This happens in business too. NASA's *Challenger* and *Columbia* disasters, the Enron and Andersen collapses, are just a few examples of organizations that lost their capacity to challenge from within and grew too comfortable. Rejecting this drift towards complacency, Toyota wants a conflict-capable culture .

The dangerous thing about being in the "dream" box is that the numbers are still good. The courageous and perceptive few who would dare to challenge the established order are told to look at the financial ratios and reminded that "You don't argue with success."

The challengers and whistleblowers either leave or submit. Numbers, however, are a lagging indicator. We need to be much more sensitive to softer signals, usually perceptible in people's behavior and energy levels.

Hell

Inevitably, the business then slips towards the "Hell" box. After so many years of neglecting and snubbing the customers (who saw that the company had stopped creating value for them long ago), it should come as no surprise that suddenly the numbers turn to red. Question: what is management's most probable answer to a sudden drop in net profit? Subsidiary question: What pressure on management does Wall Street (and other financial analysts and consultants) exert when there is a drop in profit? Once again, please think about this question *before you look at page 14.*

FIGURE 1.2 **Value matrix (artistic view)**

Cost cutting, rationalization, outsourcing, asset reallocation, divestiture—you name them, but they all boil down to the same psychological trait: *Defensiveness*. Anxiety and related defenses are part of the human condition. But as Robert Fritz points out in his book *The Path of Least Resistance*, if we are not careful we start to feel purposeless and very easily fall into a quiescent defensive state.[11]

So, after falling to Hell, companies start to play the "horizontal game." Having cut costs, the organization can indulge in the dream that things have improved since the numbers seem to prove it. Shareholders and pension funds are happy. The problem is that this symptom-driven approach has done very little to solve the real problem (that the company is neglecting its customers). Soon the symptoms are back. The company is in Hell again, and what is the answer then? A new round of cost cutting (it worked the first time so why not again?). And each time this vicious cycle is repeated we are cutting closer in towards the muscles and not into the fat anymore—to the point that, one day, the company is sold, taken over, or bankrupt. Lean is about being an athlete not a skeleton!

Do the executives of some US car manufacturer get up every day and think: "Let us destroy some value"? NO! It is the culture of "if we make it they will buy it" that destroys value for them!

How many of our businesses react to Hell by going defensive instead of courageously re-inventing themselves and striving towards Heaven again?

If the historical perspective didn't help you, maybe this strategic framework will: If businesses don't reinvent themselves, if they don't remain alert, "curious, cool, and crazy" as Hariri puts it in his *Break from the Pack* plea, they are in danger of drifting from Heaven to dream and to Hell.[12]

Our conclusions from these two insightful models are that:

- Change must be built in to businesses. As Nick van Heck often points out during seminars we run jointly, companies need to be aware not only of the journey they might undertake through the value matrix boxes, but that the matrix itself moves towards the top right-hand corner. If you don't constantly position and re-position your company, that evolution will leave you exposed in a highly competitive environment. Leaders therefore need to consider change as part of their daily routine.
- There seems to be an acceleration and major change in leadership assumptions, as shown in the historical perspective matrix.

14

■ Leaders need to move from hierarchical and content-based leadership towards creating conditions for their people to be and do their best, engaging intelligence, intuition, and passion.

THE LEADERSHIP CHALLENGE INHERENT IN THE VALUE MATRIX: THE CHANGE HOUSE

In 1996 Claes Janssen wrote *The Four Rooms of Change*, building on the transition work of Kübler-Ross (see our description in Chapter 5) and William Bridges.[13] We have taken his model and combined it with the value matrix to describe the journey that leaders must take if they are to work effectively with the matrix.

In our change work, we make an emphatic case that the journey through the change house is actually *the* critical task for senior leaders in today's challenging business landscape

While the value matrix describes perceptions of the business landscape, you can think of the change house as representing the

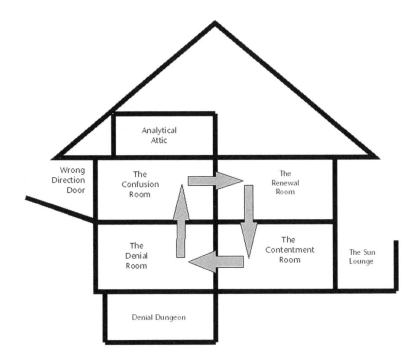

FIGURE 1.3 **The change house**

15

emotional/behavioral space that leaders need to navigate in applying the value matrix. Different parts of the organization can be in different rooms of the house at any time.

Our observations lead us to claim that there is a clockwise movement. It seems there is a learning cycle that people need to go through if they are truly to internalize change. This is definitely the case when we need to change behavior.

The renewal room equates with Heaven, the contentment room with dream, the denial room with Hell, and the confusion room with nightmare.

Each room needs its own leadership approach.

The psycho-emotional space in the renewal room is renovated, energized, focused, and purposeful. Evidence suggests that people do not stay here very long before moving into contentment, where everything feels fine for a while.

In contentment, curiosity is diminished, people seek reassurance and ignore early warning signals. The sun lounge is even worse; it is a stubbornly defended comfort zone where people protect their sun beds from foreign intruders. It is difficult to get people out of these two rooms unless there is a crisis, a burning platform, facts, data, evidence, or threats that will shake the foundations of the path of least resistance.

The denial room is aggressively defensive, blocking, projecting, actively denying data, shooting the messenger. Freud described denial as a state of "knowing-but-not-knowing," a state of irrational apprehension that inhibits appropriate action. The good news is that this is normal, but we need to get people out of here fairly quickly, to get rid of received truths, accept confusion and begin experimenting. The most challenging element here is that leaders are often attacked: "change for change sake," "ain't broke don't fix," and such catchphrases. This can be a period when leaders need all their recovery skills and techniques. Experience tells us there is no real change without strong denial at some point, so we should welcome denial as a signal that the message is hitting home.

The denial dungeon has people chained to their old habits; they can drain your energy. Trying to change this is like hitting a rubber wall: you bounce off it, it stays in place. The danger here is that the leader gives these people too much of her energy, leading to fatigue and burn out, and the dungeon members celebrate. Be aware of these people but give your energy to some warm bodies in the system, the potential early adopters.

In the confusion room people are moving on. Now looking for answers, they usually turn to the leader and demand direction: "Why didn't you tell me that before?" You did, but they were just not ready to hear.

Be alert to those in the analytic attic who keep on demanding more evidence: they are using a form of defense called rationalization and intellectualization to avoid taking the risk of changing behavior.

The wrong direction door is always a potential danger. Be ready with some early indicators of success and failure, and recognize that at times of change we sometimes hang on to things that we should have thrown out much earlier. There are many organizations whose basic weakness is that they start a lot of initiatives but don't kill any off. For many years the leaders of Sony Consumer Electronics had the slogan "Fail fast and learn from it." In Nokia R&D, the motto is "Fail faster"! Leaders need to be ready to kill something early when necessary but reward the genuine effort put in, so that people will apply their energy to new initiatives.

Rumor has it that Hewlett-Packard used to have product funerals, like an Irish wake, to celebrate effort but also to celebrate the early death of something that could have made everyone suffer.

The change house describes a leadership journey that is predictable. There is nothing mystical about it; each room needs a leadership strategy that involves the three agendas we discuss below.

THE THREE AGENDAS OF LEADERSHIP

We are living in times of accelerating change in terms of history, politics (ask business people what it was like to run a company in Poland under the Kaczynski twins), climate (any simple-minded skeptic around who doubts climate change is taking place, whatever the reasons?), the spread of knowledge (it is currently believed that a ten-year-old can know more about the world than her grandparents did), the economy (globalization, regionalization, and their political counter-reaction, nationalism), competitive pressure, etc ...

How can leaders lead under such conditions and above all, how can they ensure that their organizations stay alert, flexible, and driving the change rather than painfully adapting to it?

More than two millennia ago in Ancient Greece, Aristotle (384–322BC), a philosopher, disciple of Plato, and tutor of Alexander the Great, was working on "three modes of persuasion" in his famous rhetoric classes in the Lyceum: *logos, ethos*, and *pathos*.

Logos (intellectual agenda)

Wikipedia describes the first of these elements as follows:

> *Logos* is logical appeal and the term *logic* is derived from it. It is normally used to describe facts and figures that support the speaker's topic. Since data is difficult to manipulate, especially if from a trusted source, *logos* may sway cynical listeners. Having a *logos* appeal also enhances *ethos* because information makes the speaker look knowledgeable and prepared to his audience. However, data can be confusing and thus confuse the audience. *Logos* can also be misleading or inaccurate.[14]

We call this the intellectual or strategic agenda in business terms. When working on this agenda, engaging leaders create (or better co-create) clarity, meaning, and purpose around it. They slow down to allow time and space for their followers to build their own understanding of the new strategic intent. They allow people to play with the new concept. Such leaders have an acute sense of the needs of their "knowledge workers." They know that intelligent and talented people do not like to be given orders but need time to evaluate the new vision and propose better ways to implement it. The intellectual/strategic agenda must be robust, clear, and intellectually appealing: Who would otherwise engage wholeheartedly with something new that may seem utterly stupid? Without clarity on where we are going and why, intentions remain theoretical, PowerPoint presentations increase in number—and so do the fees paid to consultants of all types. Co-creating clarity, in a business which is in an open source environment, is fundamental. Tapping into the intellectual capital of their people is a must for leaders who want to build sustainable value.

Ethos (behavioral agenda)

Turning to the helpful Wikipedia definition of Aristotle's second mode of persuasion, we find that:

> *Ethos* is an appeal to authority. It is how well the speaker convinces the audience that he or she is qualified to speak on the particular subject. It can be done in many ways:
>
> ■ By being a notable figure in the field in question, such as a college professor or an executive of a company whose business is that of the subject.

- By having a vested interest in a matter, such as the person being related to the subject in question.
- By showing impressive *logos* that shows the audience the speaker is knowledgeable on the topic.
- By appealing to a person's ethics or character.

We call this second agenda of engaging leaders the behavioral agenda. An ethical leader ensures that her style of leadership, her displayed behavior, supports her declared intentions or her stated *logos*. Negative stories and lack of trust (on this see *The Speed of Trust: The one thing that changes everything* by Steven Covey) are among the biggest destroyers of financial value in organizations.[15] Trust is central to two of the most fundamental value drivers: speed and cost. Leaders who explicitly employ *ethos* (behavioral agenda) know which behaviors are value building, practice them, and demand feedback when they fail to do so. The behavioral agenda enables us to translate our intentions into action. *Ethos* leaders engage their people through example (Aristotle, as tutor to Alexander the Great, was the first to declare that leaders should "Walk the Talk").

Pathos (emotional agenda)

In the Wikipedia definition we read that the third mode of persuasion is:

> *Pathos*, an appeal to the audience's emotions. It can be in the form of metaphor, simile, a passionate delivery, or even a simple claim that a matter is unjust. *Pathos* can be particularly powerful if used well, but most speeches do not solely rely on *pathos*.

We call this the emotional agenda. Engaging leaders understand how to create a climate conducive to unleashing their people's passion and full potential. It is about creating conditions for people to do and be their best!

Our observations of organizations and sports tell us that the most effective emotional space provides purpose, focus, challenge and support, team spirit and identity. These spaces are not totally positive; there is some negativity but positive experiences outnumber negative by a ratio of five to one, echoing Marcial Losada and John Gottman's findings.[16] Positive emotional spaces are flourishing not languishing, they are externally focused, connect with others, and have people who display presence and focus related to a shared purpose.

When the emotional agenda is not explicit, or when it is negative or cynical, people and organizations alike tend to develop "pathologies." Leaders using *pathos* lead with energy and know how to create an emotionally engaging vision.

Charisma can probably be described as the coming together of *logos*, *ethos,* and *pathos*. It is not a permanent feature of the personality, though some seem to display it more regularly than others.

During a vacation in July 2008 in Brazil, Didier met with a Swiss Freudian psychotherapist, Marco Beata. His views as a Freudian therapist were remarkably similar to those outlined above, also building on Aristotle's rhetoric.

For Beata, the three agendas should not be viewed as separate pillars but, yes, as parts of a unique structure. The image which best fitted his views was of a volcano:

- The lava: Beata explains that everything originates and starts from emotions, and this from an early age. Like the lava of a volcano, emotions never sleep. They are sometimes hidden deep under the surface, but still boiling; sometimes more peaceful and quiet; at other times creating an unbearable pressure in the whole volcano. Everything starts with emotions!
- The body of the volcano: The mountain itself represents the intellect. It shapes, hardens, educates, and structures the emotional lava. It attempts to domesticate and channel it.
- The moments of quiet and the eruptions: These are the behavioral agenda and form the most impactful aspect of the mountain. People can see and enjoy its peaceful nature and fear its moments of anger. The behavioral agenda is a function of the two other agendas. It is however the only place from which to start observing, understanding, and getting feedback on the emotional state and structure of the whole. Change starts with the behavioral agenda.

These views are in fact complementary to Aristotle's and suggest the best way for leaders and advisors/coaches to proceed with the three agendas:

- The behaviors are the most visible part of a subject's activity. They provide useful clues on how healthy and adaptable a person—but also a team or organization—is. Working on behaviors engages people in experimenting with change and, when success appears, sustainably implementing it.

- Mirroring those behaviors and providing feedback on them make it possible to engage individuals and organizations in exploring their state of performance and how effective they are.
- However, jumping directly to the emotional agenda is often a perilous shortcut. As Marco Beata explains: "The intellect is the defense mechanism of the emotional" (see the iceberg figure we describe in Chapter 5). It is essential to start with the intellectual agenda (which is why we will start with it in the next chapter). The *logos* serves as an "intellectual gatekeeper" that must test and sanction ideas before individuals and organizations can harmoniously accept proposals for change.
- When they combine behavioral observations and feedback with intellectually compelling reasoning, leaders can successfully engage the emotional agenda of their followers.

Conclusion

The Wikipedia article on *logos*, *ethos*, and *pathos* wisely concluded: "When all three modes of persuasion are used together, a speaker or writer can create very strong arguments." Indeed, engaging leaders know that working on the three agendas at the same time is a must. Focusing on the strategic agenda alone merely creates an illusion; nothing gets done. The only thing that may (sometimes) happen is cost cutting (the easy short-term bit) but no reconstruction follows. Similarly, working hard on the behavioral agenda without setting a clear direction will ensure a team is pleasant to work in, and its leader will be extremely popular until he leads his organization into a brick wall. Note too that there is a gap between motivation and commitment or engagement. In ice hockey, *motivation* is what the coach does each time his guys enter/leave the rink: the pat on the back or the nasty remark. *Engagement* is deeper; it fires up when the three agendas are coherent. People want and look for coherence in the three agendas from their leaders; people want to *feel* meaning, not just to understand. If there is no coherence people become cynical.

Consider these comments, overheard at a public merger meeting of 1000 executives in Paris:

> "The PowerPoints were the same as they used last week for the analysts. There is no change for the internal audience, ROI, EBITDA. Did you see that customers were the last slide of 100?"

"Did you believe what he said?"

"I heard what he said but his body wasn't connected to his thoughts; he was talking flamenco but his feet weren't moving!"

"Did you see that! Those two were fighting each other publicly last week, violently, but here they are calling each other 'tu' and on a first-name basis! Did you see how Jean-Charles' mouth twisted into '*tuuu*'? Bull sh..!"

We shall now look in detail at how each of the agendas can be worked on.

CHAPTER 2

CO-CREATING CLARITY AND PURPOSE AROUND THE INTELLECTUAL AGENDA

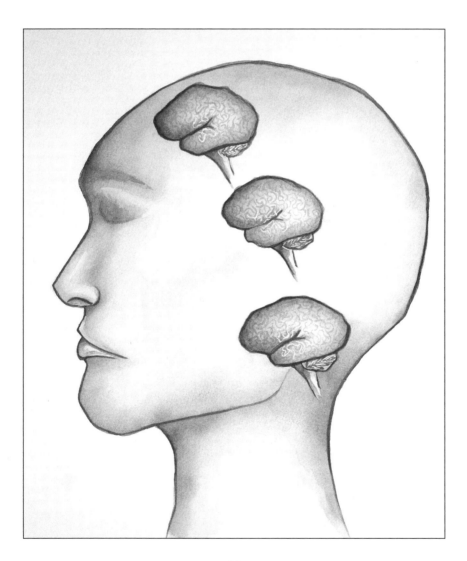

WHY VISION/MISSION/VALUES/YOU-NAME-IT STATEMENTS DON'T WORK

One of our colleagues came back, enthused and enlightened, after a long KLM flight.

At first we were puzzled. How could such enthusiasm be generated by hours of being squeezed into a space made for people four feet tall, fed with a single dry sandwich without even a diet Coke on offer (leaving aside the fact that there were of course no newspapers)? Soon, though, we realized that he wasn't talking about the airline's dubious offerings (like most so-called "frequent travelers" we know that feeling of being sneered at, manipulated, abused, and let down on our trips with most airlines). He had been electrified by a *Financial Times* article called: "My two weeks in hell with the tortured soul of Dell."[1]

Sharing the widespread frustration of those struggling to get their new laptops to function, the article's author, journalist Stefan Stern, was trying to understand the surge of anger that had overtaken him. His basic conclusion was that companies expose themselves dangerously when they flaunt exaggerated claims to their customers (hence his his deep disappointment at the difference between the company's claim and his poor experience) as well as to their own people. He ended by reminding the readers of the "built to last" research and subsequent book by Jim Collins and Jerry Porras, and in particular of one of their findings: "No company ever became visionary thanks to a vision statement."[2]

Is there an organization today which doesn't have its mission state- ment? We recently listened in awe as board members of a large European multinational discussed the vast resources they would devote to supporting the company's vision statement. The worst aspect was that when we challenged them about this, they looked at us with an air of sad complicity: "Oh yes, don't tell us! This is such a waste ... but our people need it." Really? Let's be honest: How many companies do we know where mission statements of any kind do not arouse skepticism and suspicion among the employees?

As Stefan Stern points out, the biggest danger with such statements is that people (inside or outside) will take the promise for granted and hold you to account for it. How many of us would have the same courage and integrity as the board members of one of the world's most famous drinks companies, who claimed to take their Behavioral Chart so seriously that any director who failed to rate satisfactorily on it would step down? The members of the board lived up to that promise. Those whose 360° results weren't as good as expected "felt the heat," and were promptly coached to improve on their value-building behaviors. DSM, the famous Dutch firm providing "innovative products and services in life sciences and material sciences," has implemented a leadership development process that makes a significant distinction: "Competencies describe potential but behavior is what we do."

Mission statements should be aspirational (tending towards or declaring an intention) and inspirational (that is, leaving space for people to position themselves in it) but not over prescriptive, politically correct, or polished to the point of lacking sense, integrity, and authenticity.

We recently worked with a Scandinavian energy firm which had been carefully considering how to choose value statements and, once they were identified, how to ensure they would be owned and lived by the people. From the discussion, two plausible but very different approaches emerged. The first of these was based on the situational leadership model. The leaders in the room felt that, if the company was under extreme pressure and people were asking for clear directions, it would be perfectly acceptable—indeed desirable—for the board to indicate what behaviors and ethics would be expected from themselves and their people. However, they said, this would also require a heavy investment in "selling" the guidelines to the staff, who wouldn't, by definition, have been consulted. The second approach would be to lead a discussion throughout the organization of the behaviors and values that were most admired in the firm, and so to identify the desired aspirational values. That would take longer, but once the goals were identified they would be faster to implement.

When considering how to implement—"communicate"—the future value statement, the leaders drew on their own experience and the research they had commissioned. They concluded that the most credible and efficient way to communicate was by direct contact. People believe in their peers far more than in corporate communications, so a "viral marketing" type of process was unanimously decided on. Viral marketing is in fact the label that the company gives to the "personal" engagement processes.

CO-CREATING CLARITY AND MEANING

"Are we all clear?" asks the CEO after PowerPointing his audience to death.

What is the most likely answer, if any? A resounding and often bored: YES! There isn't a more stupid question to be asked than that one!

Biologist Francisco Varela observed: "Less than 20 percent of the information we use to create a perception is external to the brain. Information from the outside only perturbs a system; it never functions as objective instructions."[3] In other words, 80 percent of the information we will use is already present in our brains (as experience, knowledge, beliefs) before we listen to someone's argument and decide upon it. And in any case, new information coming from outside ourselves may be perceived as disturbing and is therefore likely to be blocked, denied, or suppressed.

It is widely accepted that our brain can process 500 words a minute. However, an effective presenter may only speak 125 words a minute. What happens to all that spare capacity? Since information from the outside perturbs our system, the odds are that we are: a) planning our next vacation, b) thinking of that urgent mail/meeting/PowerPoint/ reply to send, c) trying to resolve a domestic issue, d) preparing a rebuff to what we are hearing ... Listening, you said?

So how can we create clarity and meaning? Let's turn to Varela again:

It isn't the ability to solve problems that makes an organization smart. It is the ability of its members to enter into a world whose significance they share. If everyone in the group thinks that what is occurring is significant (even as they have different perspectives) then they don't have to convince one another. They can act rapidly, creatively, and in concert.[4]

This is co-creating clarity and meaning.

An example of successful co-creation

A few years ago, we sneaked into the annual convention of the top 200 people of a European bank: Two days of PowerPoint sessions, HR-planted questions for the traditional Q&As, a completely apathetic audience. The only thing missing was the pre-recorded canned laughter of the audience that you hear in the brain-dead series/sitcoms that TV channels around the world bore us with.

Our undiplomatic reply when asked what we thought of it unexpectedly got us invited to the next year's event. And it is true that things had improved: there were good intentions (getting participants to react, though still to PowerPoint presentations). There was rather more energy and a feeling of something significantly better and new for the participants.

Alas, between those two sessions we'd been invited by a creative Spanish executive, Jose Luis Martinez, who was heading the Nokia Mobile Phones' Spanish commercial arm at the time, to observe how he was running a true engagement process. A new segmentation model had been decided on centrally and the local offices were required to implement it. Martinez felt that it would be hopeless to try to engage his organization with this change by email; that would just produce pretty much the atmosphere described above. Instead, he decided to close down the office for a few days and invite the whole organization (150 people) to "take ownership of it through co-creating clarity."

In the two and a half days that the convention lasted, there were just 60 minutes of PowerPoint and other video clips. For the rest of the time, Martinez had prepared his management team members to animate discussions, provoke debates, and invite challenges and feedback so that the participants would co-create clarity, meaning, and purpose behind this new model. Structuring the process flexibly and constantly adapting to the audience's response, and adopting a highly supportive style to encourage any junior staff who felt intimidated in the early stages, Jose Luis and his team managed to engage their audience in effective, courageous, exploratory discussions. By making themselves approachable and vulnerable, the management team reduced distance and increased their credit in the "emotional bank account."

One vivid memory we have of the convention was a discussion we overheard among several secretaries as they were leaving. They were talking about the encouraging responses to their questions, and one of them suddenly challenged her colleagues to meet on Monday to follow up on the session. Given their understanding of the new segmentation model, she proposed they look for better ways to deal with the company's clients that they had spotted on the new grid. "Different needs require different processes" were the last words we heard before dashing out to the airport.

Engaging leaders create time and space for people to "play" with the new reality. They create the conditions for people to *explore* prior to making conclusions. They take personal risks by laying their cards on the table, make themselves and their strategic intent approachable. People cannot integrate or own a new plan if they are not given the space to do so.

In Toyota goals are purposefully broad. "If the goals are too concrete and specific, employees will not be able to achieve their full potential," or "In painting with broad strokes we allow employees to channel their energies in different directions and force specialists from different disciplines to collaborate."[5]

Different people need different things to co-create clarity and meaning

The Myers–Briggs Type Indicator (MBTI), based on Jung's archetype theory, identifies four temperaments. People of different temperaments will look at different aspects of a situation or proposal in order to create clarity, but will all need the time and space we referred to earlier, though they will use it in different ways.[6] The temperaments and their approaches are:

- *NTs*: Rationalists, bringing the development of strategies, design, long-term thinking. They achieve progress where there is competence and knowledge, and therefore need time and space to explore and make sense of the purpose, context, and strategic intent of a new project.
- *SJs*: Guardians, bringing standardization, structure, caution, clarity. They feel confident where they have security, and therefore need time and space to look at all the details, facts, and figures if they are to commit themselves to a new project.
- *SPs*: Experts, bringing energy, action, solving problems and crises. They are adaptable if they have freedom, and therefore need time and space to play with a new idea, to "trial and error it" so that they can make sense of it.
- *NFs*: Idealists, bringing harmony, coordination, and development of people. They are catalysts if they are allowed to behave authentically, and therefore need time and space to understand how a new decision will affect people and impact on their values and culture.

Whatever the temperaments we are working with, people are smart: they do things for their own unique and rational reasons. They act and perceive things in ways that support their current view or sense of the world. There is always some personal logic behind action; the problem is that the logic is not immediately accessible even to the person who takes the action. Brain researcher Jeffrey Gray has argued that much behavior is not conscious: we become aware after the act. He estimates that consciousness of action lags behind action by about one-fifth of a second in our daily lives.[7]

Sometimes, to show our audience how complete misunderstanding can result when people assume things are clear, we like to play one of those "stupid tricks." It goes like this: Ask the audience (and the extroverts in particular) to *silently* think of a sport which starts with a tee (pronounced "T"). Explain that it is an obvious choice, that it was once considered an elite sport but is now played by thousands around the world and is very popular. To clarify, add that the main stars have historically come from Europe and the United States, and that we probably all know the names of some men and women champions. Ask the audience if they are clear (obviously!) about the sport in question and ask them to remain *silent*. Instruct them then to close their eyes and slowly mimic the attitude of someone playing that sport. When all eyes are closed and postures adopted, ask them to open their eyes.

Surprise is guaranteed when the participants, who are all posed as tennis players (sometimes table tennis or tai-chi), discover you teeing off in a golfer's posture. Golf starts with a tee and Tennis with a "T" ... Stupid yes, and very illustrative of what happens when, however full of good intentions, someone tries to impose, sell, offer a personal vision, intellectual concept, and understanding to others. To the question: "All clear?" we will get a resounding "Yes!"—and everybody goes off to do different things.

As Nick van Heck suggests: "It is much less about hoping to find the right answer than having an engagement process around the creation of strategic clarity."

Reality is a social construction

Reality is constructed in the language we use every day. We need to explore the social constructions that individuals and groups are using if we are to understand their reality and their implicit assumptions.

Some years ago one of the authors was working with the senior leadership team of a famous biscuit/cookie manufacturer. They were complaining about the lack of energy and enthusiasm in the management layer directly below them: "unmotivated second-rate people." It did not take long to uncover the problem: the board's language. What they spoke about, more than anything else, was EBITDA, not customers, quality, or availability.[8] Every meeting was dominated by financial concerns, understood or misunderstood. Why? The executive board had been hired by a venture capital firm to get the business to a selling point in two years and their bonuses were EBITDA based. EBITDA was their motivation but it was received cynically by the layer below.

Explore, co-create, and conclude

As far as we know, no one has ever attempted to quantify the financial value wasted in sterile debates amongst executives.

Intelligent and competent people tend to build "models" about everything very quickly. It is one of the capacities which differentiate us from animals. Modeling the world is a useful mental process which enables us to understand what is happening, compare it to our existing mental models, communicate them to others, and hopefully agree on a course of action. Many psychologists argue that our consciousness is actually a comparator of modeled expectations with what actually happened.

This "natural gift" also has its downside. Humans tend to attach themselves to the models they have mentally constructed. One of the reasons is to be found in Francisco Varela's work quoted earlier. Seeing our mental models challenged may result in fear (when the challenge undermines a model which supports our comfort, our deeply held beliefs), anger (when we feel that somebody else's model competes with ours or disrespects our patiently built mental architectural jewel), disengagement (when we think the other person's model is too remote from our reality or inferior to our own brilliant conception), or various other forms of rejection. Yet as the 17th-century English priest T. Fuller once said: "Contradiction should awaken attention not passion." Our attention is present when we can attach, include, and digest the new information in something meaningful to us. When we cannot, we reject it.

Scottish therapist John McWhirter, when teaching on the University of Valence's Masters in Intervention Psychology program, likes to quote a recent finding on how the human brain reacts to differences: "The human brain operates on differential systems."[9] McWhirter considers this a fundamental discovery. In his view, it explains why the natural inclination of human beings in discussions is to "use their brain as a weapon instead of a tool": the attention of participants in a discussion will be raised faster and more strongly when the topics, ideas, suggestions, and beliefs expressed conflict with their own views. This helps explain why executives seem to spend so much time in their meetings on the points of disagreement, endlessly arguing about those rather than seeking to build bridges from the areas of agreement. In a 2001 review of all the literature on human conditioning, Baumeister and colleagues concluded that "bad is stronger than good": perceived threats or challenges get more of our energy and attention than reward.[10] They argue that this is a vestige of our animal brain; the vestigial monkey is still as powerful as ever when threats arise, but for the most part its influence is exerted at a subconscious level .

In our experience, in effective discussions people's attitudes will pass through three stages:

- *Exploring*: It is vital to understand the particular and specific context in which the other parties made their assumptions, built their model, and took a decision, if we are to ensure a meaningful discussion. Since our mind "double processes," as seen above, when the other party talks and unwittingly triggers our "difference-seeking sensors," we are immediately tempted to object with our own models, personal experience, opinions, and so on. Since childhood, the role models that have been held up to us are the people who can come to a conclusion faster than others (in school for example) and take decisions faster and better. We are trained to be "conclusion-drawing machines" and are evaluated in those terms. Yet exploration requires us to let go of our own models and thoughts for a moment, to be able to fully understand and empathize with the other person's point of view. Some of the ancient Eastern self-defense techniques teach nothing else: do not attempt to block an attack, use your opponent's influx, energy, and dynamics.
- *Co-creating*: Skilled dialogue is not a succession of more or less respected points of views being laid out. Successful negotiators master the art of engaging all parties in building a solution which provides them all with a sense of being respected (so that egos don't get in the way) and ensures that everybody can walk away with clarity and a sense of having had their key needs attended to. The purpose here is to move, as Collin and Porras said, from the "either-or" mentality to the "both-and" one. The co-creation process is fundamental in gaining an emotional commitment to the change desired rather than a simplistic and neutral "intellectual buy-in 'coz I can't find arguments against it any more..." Indeed, in using language like "buy-in" we may already be putting up barriers for many people who are already prepared buy the idea! Leaders can try to legislate for many things, but not commitment and engagement.

■ *Concluding*: It is only at that point, after co-creating and getting emotional commitment, that people will be ready to go out and implement the changes. There will be as many ways of interpreting and making change happen as there are people. Expect no single total alignment. However, having clearly defined the boundaries and rules of engagement in the concluding part, change leaders can be assured that movement will take place in the right direction, with some deviations here and there but no breaking of the key constraints or rules.

Alas, too often, very intelligent people engulf themselves in a different process:

■ *Stating/selling/advocating*: With the best of intentions, the most forceful or inspired leader suggests a course to follow, a model to adhere to. Very quickly, the relative skepticism, the questions, the doubts, the fears—sometimes the cynicism—of the others will put him in a position of defending the initial input, which will little by little become "his." From selling, some may fall into advocating, ready to use any flawed logic to fight their corner. This brings us to the next level of value-destroying discussions.
■ *Imposing/closing down*: After minutes, hours, days, sometimes months or years of unfruitful arguments, the leader(s) or the group, frustrated by the lack of process, will call for the imposition of one decision. Rarely do they reach the best outcome in this type of closure. It is reactive, frustration driven, not value building any more.
■ *Conflict/neutrality/submission*: The impact of the previous step is predictable, even when it is the participants themselves who seem to have demanded that a final decision be imposed on them. Some will be upset, because they intuitively sense that the wrong outcome has been decided, or because they feel disrespected/insignificant or that their concern hasn't been addressed. They will go into conflict mode, sometimes openly (a blessing—at least we know something went wrong), sometimes covertly (spreading negative stories and rumors, being pessimistic, trivializing the change or decision made, sometimes sabotaging). Some others will "mentally check-out" and switch off their creative energy; this has been described as "presenteeism" (physically present but mentally absent). In some cases, they are already on the phone to headhunters, and in many cases they operate on a "just enough to keep the boss happy" basis. What a waste of potential. Finally, others will be so scared and discouraged that they

will fall into a submissive mode, blindly obedient, spending most of their energy trying to guess what the boss wants to hear, and avoiding any risks that might put them in the limelight.

Some years ago one of the authors was invited by the sales director of a major beverages business to come in and "fix" his team. The members were not delivering on what they promised, European forecasts were off by 5 to 15 percent every quarter, and he was under pressure to make them perform to target. The interviews unveiled the simple truth early on: the director was so dominant and controlling (a "drainpipe leader") that the rule became: "Don't argue with him, say yes to his numbers to take the heat off, and we can avoid any fallout." This pattern had been repeating itself for a year, and missed forecasts were affecting the company's share price.

GUESSING THE FUTURE OR GETTING READY FOR IT?

A serious and misleading consequence of the way our "concluding minds" function is the desperate pursuit of the illusory "right strategy." How much energy is spent in search of the perfect strategy as a result of this misconception?

Flexibility, "fail fast," the value-creation state of mind (as opposed to the defensive value-capture focus) are crucial in today's converging environments.

When we work with Nick van Heck on his "scenario exploring" process, we invite as large as possible a group of executives (100, 300, 500) of the same organization into a room. The key message from Nick is that "strategy is not about guessing the future but preparing for it": in other words, enabling your people and organization to be strategic at all times. Instead of fixing their minds on "finding the right answer," Nick throws the participants into a scenario exploration process. The idea is to let them understand what their business is truly about. What are the value drivers? What could happen to them tomorrow if ...? By engaging in a scenario exploration, participants build collective clarity and intelligence (as well, by the way, as more personal and trust-conducive relationships).

When the business drivers and the scenarios which impact upon them have been explored and clarified, the participants seek to identify the early warning signals from the external environment that would prompt the company to opt for one scenario or another. In that way, a major part of the organization has analyzed the possible future options and the signals which might indicate that one or the other needs to be adopted, and can take action without having to wait for decisions to move up and down the long chain of command. We have already spoken of how trust impacts on cost and speed; here is a great example of how to increase the trust level in an organization

"Strategy is too important to be left in the hands of strategists" is Nick van Heck's conclusion when he talks about leadership engagement in the context of strategy.

When we interviewed a board member in a large bank about how it was deciding its new strategy (which was supposed to result in support for the change process we'd been asked to bring about), his reply was unequivocal: "With top-notch consultants and secretly of course. A strategy is too important to be shared with everybody!"

It is this elitist vision of strategy that successful engaging leaders manage to challenge and overturn. It is not strategies that make for success but their implementation. Accenture stated in their 2003 *Innovating for the Upturn* report: "The real test is not whether a company has been smartest about predicting the timing of the recovery, but whether it has been truly competitive in its preparation."

James Surowiecki is an American journalist who regularly contributes to *The New Yorker*, where he writes a column on finance. In 1995, he authored an excellent book, *The Wisdom of Crowds*.[11] Starting with a failed experiment by a British scientist at the beginning of the last century, Surowiecki cites numerous cases where the mass of non-experts were found to be far more reliable and better at guessing the answers than the so-called experts.[12]

LEADING EDGE ORGANIZATIONS IDENTIFY AND ADDRESS THEIR STRATEGIC DILEMMAS

A lot has already been written about strategic dilemmas. Amongst the reflections most applicable to business, those of Joseph Badaracco, and of Fons Trompenaars and Charles Hampden-Turner are the most useful.[13]

Badaracco cites the dilemma posed by Jean-Paul Sartre, the famous French writer and philosopher, in a play first performed in 1948.[14] In the play Hugo Barine, a young idealist, has to face a harsh choice: Whether to kill a party traitor and so fulfill his political ideals, or to keep his romantic dream alive and not "dirty his hands" with the blood of another fellow human being.

Historically, business leaders have taken a simplistic approach to dilemmas, a linear and straightforward one. The problem with dilemmas, however, is that they do not go away: they keep coming back, not necessarily in the same form but with the same principles at stake. The more complex our business environment becomes, the less successful is the linear approach.

Senior leaders have fundamental dilemmas built into their role. The three parallel business agendas of delivering today, aggressive continuous improvement, and building the future are omnipresent. Juggling with them poses daily dilemmas. An increasing number of leading organizations are grappling with multiple, opposing problems and tensions that need to be addressed at the same time. This is dilemma management: the leader's ability to lead her organization through these conflicting pressures, again and again. For many, the way you handle dilemmas becomes your core signature of leadership.

For most of us, part of our success formula (and the secret of promotion) is our capacity to spot problems and solve them as they appear. In an "engineering perspective," a problem has to have a solution; therefore it can and must be solved. Simple businesses have problems not dilemmas.

Dilemmas can be thought of as having two axes (horizontal and vertical) which seem to express incompatible goals. For example:

- ensuring the business's sustainability whilst shaping a highly flexible organization
- providing strong leadership whilst building ownership/responsibility amongst employees
- having a clear vision whilst feeling at ease with ambiguity and uncertainty
- managing for profits whilst putting people first
- thinking long term whilst surviving the dictatorship of "the quarterly results."

The three business agendas of delivering today, aggressive and continuous improvement, and building the future are, when they are present together, dilemma generators.

Dilemma management can be described as having various characteristics:

- It moves from "either–or" to "both–and." It is not about choosing which axis is better but being able to understand how to make both work.
- It is recurrent: one doesn't necessarily "solve" a dilemma. It is

something that keeps on coming back, for which the answers and the ingredients (a bit more of the "x" axis this time, a bit more of "y" the next) evolve in relation to the context.

■ It addresses (rather than solving) two issues which seem to be conflicting.

■ It is a very powerful way to re-engage people who had previously been de-energized by an either–or decision.

■ It is appropriate in today's world of complexity and adaptation.

Where are the dilemma conversations taking place in your organization?

A simple way to assess and work with dilemmas inside your organization is to follow those four steps:

■ Step 1: Identify that you have a dilemma:
  – Describe its horns/aspects.
  – Show how it is different from a problem that can be fixed.
■ Step 2: Explore the dilemma:
  – How is it a challenge for you?
  – How are you dealing with it now?
  – What would others say about the way you're coping with it?
■ Step 3: Now that you've explored this dilemma:
  – How are you seeing it differently?
  – What options are emerging?
  – What is the best balance between the aspects of the dilemma?
■ Step 4: Action:
  – What will you do to manage it?
  – Who do you need to influence?
  – When will you need to revisit it?
  – What will indicate that you need a fresh approach to its ongoing management?

Here is a recent example of how one of our colleague's clients addressed dilemma management:

A major UK hospital wanted to achieve financial independence from the UK Ministry of Health. In order to do so, it needed to balance its books, eliminating any losses by the end of the financial year (which in the UK runs from April to March).

Financial independence (Trust Status) was critical to the hospital's strategic plans, which included being in shape to merge with a world-class medical university and another hospital. All this started with balancing the books and gaining freedom to do so.

In January, with three months to go, the hospital was running a 15 percent deficit for the year. The board decided to cut and cut hard. A month later the deficit had increased by several percent! Why? It really felt as if the leadership team were pulling levers that were not connected to anything.

The issue was not that people were unwilling to cut costs. Everyone had signed up to becoming financially independent. It just went "against the grain" for a community who were passionate about patient care to cut patient services: "I agree with this, but you don't mean me in Renal do you?" It was so counter-cultural that some of the top team were on long-term sick leave.

We posed the question and helped uncover the hidden part of the dilemma. How to cut costs *and* do this in the context of the values of the organization? When people engaged with this question the savings came quickly. They cut HR, IT, and all other non-patient, non-front-line services to the bone. The books were balanced and the hospital gained Trust Status. The financial situation was turned around and the savings were made for the year in less than eight weeks.

The leaders had to re-visit this dilemma once they were financially independent, in order to re-balance operations after such drastic action and re-invest in the support services they had cut. The top team had a lot more freedom to do this because of the financially freer position they were in, and they were quickly able to adjust the balance.

DSM in the Netherlands is a company whose senior management has successfully addressed major dilemmas over the last four decades.

The title DSM (Dutch State Mines) precisely described the original company and its operations. Today it is world famous for its material science, nutrition products and services, celebrated for its role in the World Food Program, and driving breakthroughs in "nutriceuticals." Its Dyneema product range is saving lives everywhere. The present and previous chairmen/CEOs and management teams are modest people but they have put a strategic dialogue process in place which, by its very nature, has exposed evolutionary dilemmas. The process allows people to go successfully (though not painlessly) through the process of dilemma exploration described above. It is no surprise that the company logo—

38

"Unlimited DSM"—expresses the beliefs and feelings of its employees, because they have experienced what it means in the course of many fundamental changes.

CONCLUSION

Engaging leaders invite their people to engage with the intellectual/strategic agenda by creating space and time for them to explore, understand, and build their own sense and meaning around a new direction. This is difficult to achieve through coercion or imposition (though these are sometimes needed in times of crisis that the organization cannot otherwise respond to). It is not about asking the organization to act like consultants; it is about co-creating transparency, meaning, and understanding which will allow people to take their destiny in their own hands, to become purposeful instead of being thrown into a reactive state by competitors. Co-creating clarity on the intellectual agenda is no longer an option that can be ignored in today's dynamic environment. Tapping into the collective intelligence of your teams and enabling it to be freely expressed is essential if you want to get your organization firmly anchored in the "Heaven" box of the value matrix!

CHAPTER 3

BUILDING ECONOMIC VALUE THROUGH THE APPROPRIATE LEADERSHIP STYLE (THE BEHAVIORAL AGENDA)

PEOPLE LISTEN TO WHAT YOU DO!

We were once in a meeting that was addressed by a wise senior Citibanker. "People don't listen to what you say, they listen to what you do!" he told us. To prove his point, he asked: "Please do as I tell you," then touched the top of his head and said: "Touch your skull." Everyone did so. "Please touch your forehead," he said, doing so himself, while we all followed suit. "Please touch your nose." We all obeyed, wondering where he was taking us ... Then he said "Please touch your neck," and put his finger on his chin. Most of us went for the chin too.

He apologized for the simplicity of the demonstration and closed by reinforcing his point on the importance of behaviors and ethics. "People will scrutinize everything you do or don't do and use it as a cue to perform or underperform."

Each and every day intelligent, well-meaning leaders and workers destroy or create value for themselves and their companies. Almost always, in our experience, the value destruction is unintentional.[1]

Even today, people remember Gerald Ratner's speech in 1991 as a classic example of how inappropriate behavior can cause massive value destruction. The unfortunate Ratner, CEO of a highly successful chain of jewelers, boasted that his company could sell a decanter and set of glasses for £4.95 "because it's total crap!" That remark, picked up by the press, almost instantaneously wiped half a billion pounds off the company's value on the stock exchange. And every day, this (in)famous example is reflected in other cases.

We were recently asked to facilitate a strategy session for the "cash cow" division of a client of ours. We had been warned that a very bright but "difficult" character would be present. It was truly sad to see how such an intelligent and knowledgeable individual had managed to become his own worst enemy and how much harm he was doing to the company, whilst at the same time full of self-confidence and trying hard to create value.

He was one of the world's most highly respected specialists in his area and was fascinating to listen to. At first we wondered why someone like this was still vegetating several grades away from a board position. It didn't take long to understand: in the strategic debate that we were facilitating, he quickly started to lay down the law, patronizing his boss, contradicting his colleagues, and projecting arrogant superiority towards all. Not really the way to get to the top. Our attempts to help him become more effective were met by aggressiveness and cynicism. We remember leaving the meeting with a sense of sadness: why was the man doing this to himself? His behavior made it impossible for his colleagues (and the organization as a whole) to realize how brilliant he actually was. Because his attitude was so inappropriate, he was condemning himself to nothing more than a "specialist" role. From time to time he was called in because the senior managers needed to "pick his brains," but then he would be sent back to the outer darkness.

His contribution to the team was a mixed blessing. On the one hand, his incisive comments supported by deep knowledge and experience often helped the team move forward. On the other hand, he would talk to the point of rambling for long periods, interrupt his colleagues without bothering to listen to their proposals, leap in to challenge everything that anyone said. His style prevented any exploration of ideas and led to ugly battles over the conclusions arrived at. After an hour of this, the discussion was completely deadlocked. We understood better why facilitators were needed there.

CREATING AND DESTROYING VALUE THROUGH BEHAVIORS

Most of the behavior that causes value destruction is totally unconscious, and those who engage in it are oblivious of its effects. We were recently invited by a high-tech company to help shake up its team of top designers. It was agreed we would first attend the monthly, day-long meeting of their worldwide management team, not contributing ourselves but simply observing the dynamics taking place. The most obvious moment of value destruction (apart from the classic swathe of open laptops, the pretences of listening, the displays of multi-tasking capability when one of their colleagues was presenting her summary of activities for the month) came in the afternoon. Two promising young engineers were invited to present the projects they wanted to get funded.

From the start, it was obvious they were intimidated by the seniority of the audience (all three to four grades senior to them), which showed a complete lack of interest. The seniors hardly seemed to have noticed their presence. Nobody even bothered to ask them to sit and so they stood like children in primary school waiting for their turn to recite in front of the class. As soon as the first one started making an apparently very well-prepared case, a barricade of laptops went up in front of him. Nobody seemed to pay attention to his presentation. He went through an increasingly nervous monologue for 15 minutes. When he had finished, he asked the audience if they had any questions. The leader looked up from an important email to reply: "No question. Next!"

The next applicant tried harder to gain their attention, varied the tone and pitch, tried to move away from the PowerPoint style, but without much more success. Fifteen minutes later, having been granted a sizeable budget for their project, these two rising stars were sent back to their own world. One of our colleagues unobtrusively followed them out of the room to ask their impression of the "Almighty Gods." You can imagine what he found. Even though their request for funding had been accepted, they were shocked, disappointed, and totally demotivated by such an ocean of uninterest, and resented the sense of total disrespect and arrogance shown by their bosses' bosses' bosses.

The next day, when we confronted them over this, the senior leaders were shocked. None of them denied what had happened and suddenly the penny dropped: Though they had been acting with the best of intentions (responding as quickly as possible to the dozens of high-priority emails they had received), they had emptied their emotional bank account with those two young engineers, and most probably with many others who would have heard the story on "corridor radio" in the past 24 hours.

Leaders tend to underestimate the impact their behavior has down the line. Though it may seem a minor example, we can't forget one particular incident. We were sitting in a meeting with the board of a Swiss pharmaceutical company and, several times during the discussion, one of the leaders of the group jabbed a finger towards a colleague and asserted: "That's not the point!" Insignificant as it might seem, this simple "micro-behavior" was either raising tension or completely shutting the discussion off. When we gave him our feedback about that, he of course maintained we were making a big fuss over a trivial detail. We pointed out that, given who he was, this would soon become the "cool style" in management meetings, a suggestion he flatly denied. Two weeks later, we were facilitating a meeting with people whose direct bosses had not even been in the board meeting. The "that's not the point" (and related body language) had become the norm when somebody meant to challenge or even simply refocus the discussion. One of us quickly took the elevator to the top floor and invited the finger-jabbing board member to come for a sneak look. He was flabbergasted! Executives tend to forget how closely they are scrutinized by their employees.

On another occasion, one of the authors was present when a team of highly motivated senior executives made a presentation to a board member. They were reporting the results of a business improvement project designed to open up creative pathways into emerging markets. The project team members were wired and good, with lots of brain power and 200 years of experience between them. Unfortunately, the board member was not a fluent speaker of English. He had a set response to anything he disagreed with: "Don't dream!" After hearing this just four times, this experienced team were thoroughly demoralized— dreaming was exactly what they had been doing with some success. The board member was unaware of his verbal tic and did not understand the effect it was having; he even remarked to the team that they seemed to lose energy part way through their presentation and that they should do something about that! He later listened to our feedback about it, but did not act upon it. The same pattern continued.

On the other hand, there are many positive illustrations of value/ reputation building behaviors:

- Serge Trigano, the founder/owner of Club Med, made a point of dropping in on his "villages" just at the time when new clients (members) were arriving at the hotel. The result was quite amusing to watch, with all the employees dashing to get his luggage while he was running ahead of the clients to carry theirs, to prove the point that clients should be priority number one.
- Derek Abel, when he was Dean of IMD, was determined to send out the message of excellence and respect at all levels. When he heard a student had behaved discourteously to a waitress in the lunch room, he made it a point to go there at lunchtime the next day, call for silence, comment on the event, publicly apologize to the waitress in the name of the school, and give the student 24 hours to make a public apology or leave. The lady's relief and evident pride showed that she really felt IMD was committed to excellence and respect.
- Barry Wilson, as CEO of Medtronic Europe, asked us to arrange an event for 400 members of the company's European headquarters and its Swiss plant in Tolochenaz. The objective was to improve relations between the expatriate headquarters personnel and the staff of the plant. We designed a set of activities taking up several decks of a steamer on Lake Geneva. The participants were in two competing teams, each with a quite complex hierarchy in which, of course, the junior staff were in charge and the bosses would follow their instructions. In the heat of the moment one employee (a political asylum seeker) got so carried away with Barry's failure to make a simple container to carry raw eggs between the decks that he threw a cup of

coffee at him, giving an interesting new look to Barry's otherwise impeccable white shirt and Hermes tie.

The poor man was probably ready to throw himself in the lake when he realized what he'd done. But during the plenary review, Barry invited him on stage with a huge smile, recounted the incident with humor and gave it a positive twist ("Thank you for your passion!"). That gesture did more to break down the barriers than anything else during that day.

■ One of the most impressive demonstrations of value building through appropriate behaviors and leadership style was shown by two companies involved in supplying high-technology machine tools. The relationship, which could have been a simple client–supplier contract with one firm building the hardware and the other the software, rapidly evolved towards partnership. There were passionate and uncompromising characters on the boards of both companies. Those leaders rapidly realized that, while their strategic agenda was clear and sound (between them they had captured more than 50 percent of their market against household-name Asian competitors), there was a risk that their sometimes abrasive management styles might begin to disrupt progress. Some of their subordinates were already (not surprisingly) beginning to copy their methods. The leaders decided to work seriously on their behavior patterns. In a spectacular turnaround, they went from "using their minds as weapons" to "using their minds as tools": the highly intelligent and knowledgeable head of R&D continued to push his points with passion and strength, but started to invite and welcome push-back from his colleagues and subordinates. The CFOs, who had tended to "sit on the fence" and watch the collective boat sink in endless discussions, decided to take charge and actively build bridges and clarity during meetings. In six months, the tensions that had threatened to hinder the companies' cooperation were resolved, and the partnership developed into what became virtually one combined firm, even though both enterprises remained completely independent legally and financially.

POSITIVE AND NEGATIVE STORIES

We once did some work for a client who wanted to understand why stories in some parts of the organization seemed to be more positive, inspiring, and hopeful than in others. After studying various areas with

47

positively and negatively loaded cultures, we found one interesting fact. The main difference was that in the positive organizations people reported that their leaders' behaviors, styles, and attitudes reflected their values and strategic intent. In other words, there was a strong perception that the behavioral and intellectual agendas were aligned. The opposite was true for the more cynical, negative organizations. The good old "walk the talk" in a sense. Remember Aristotle: When *ethos* does not support *logos*, pathologies arise.

But this is only the visible part of the iceberg. Engaging leaders don't simply walk the talk, they mobilize others through specific behavior.

When Chris was OB and leadership professor at IMD and Cranfield, he went through all the literature about value-building and value-destroying behaviors. He came back with eight core behaviors which, when practiced by leaders, cascade down and foster the state of mind needed to build organizations that can flourish in converging environments.

THE EIGHT VALUE-BUILDING BEHAVIORS

Our long experience in working with teams all over the world, in whatever kind of national culture and at whatever level, shows that there are eight behaviors which can be directly linked to higher performance:

- Listen actively.
- Ask open questions.
- Summarize.
- Support and constructively challenge.
- Clarify.
- Ask for time-out.
- Give feedback/run a review.

In this section, we are dealing with "challenging" and "supporting" under a single heading, although they are separate behaviors.

Listen actively

Active listening is very different from "politely shutting-up while the other person's talking and waiting for the right time to make my point." Active listening moves people from:

- *Blunt assertions* to *exploration*: As we saw, our success formula is constantly challenged here. This is not about becoming tentative and doubtful, it is about reflecting on the context before coming to conclusions.

■ *Judging* to *seeking to understand*: This is about withholding judgment and trying to understand why another concept of the world is being presented. It is about "looking for the golden nugget" in the other person's argument, not confirming your own position.

■ *Provoking* to *challenging positively*: Too often, human beings take up fixed positions in a discussion. Abandoning that position and challenging rather than provoking helps a great deal.

■ *Assuming to clarifying*: How many historical and business disasters have been caused by the tendency of humans to make quick assumptions? As the war movie *A Bridge Too Far* reminds us, it is important to be clear about the assumptions/implicit models that people are acting on.[2] The first NASA Mars probe missed the planet completely despite intensive preparations on two continents that added up to thousands of years of work. The truth emerged after the biggest software audit in history: the joint US–European teams were using different measuring systems on different sides of the pond, one metric the other Imperial, each assuming the other was following suit, and only checking when it was too late.

Active listening encourages people to contribute by:

■ enabling a variety of personal opinions and perceptions to contribute to decision making
■ giving confidence to explore alternatives constructively
■ being affirmative to others
■ establishing the basis for effective feedback and clarity building.

Ask open questions

Some successful people have a reputation of being quick decision makers, great at bringing things to a conclusion. For them exploration through open questioning seems slow, indecisive, and a show of weakness. In today and tomorrow's converging environments, however, the quality of exploration and questioning will be a massive competitive advantage.

Sometimes, too, these decisive leaders may steer discussions by using judgmental statements disguised as questions ("So how can we do it?"

"Why are you so negative?" or "Why do you always disagree?" are not open questions). Marcial Losada's work on micro-behavior in successful teams has shown that it is empathic open questions that make the difference; he defines this as showing interest in and attending to the response. Empathic questions build the connections that give shared energy and identity.

Asking open questions allows us to:

- fully explore other people's ideas and suggestions
- discover how others feel about ideas and decisions, testing commitment
- explore alternatives
- stimulate creativity
- create a climate of enquiry rather than advocacy.

Summarize

In a good, strategic discussion, someone should summarize every 7–12 minutes where we are, what the agreement is/is not, what ground has been covered or remains open, and so on. Summarizing is part of the energizing process of the debate: Listening actively and asking open questions contribute to the exploration dynamic, while summarizing focuses the debate and is part of the concluding dynamic (even if only temporarily). Summarizing also helps to keep your mind busy and prevents you drifting into other ideas, so it is a powerful way to support active listening skills. It ensures that everyone is aware of the points they agree and disagree on; it contributes to creating quality. Summarizing is the primary tool for building common or shared views, and is also the foundation for support and constructive challenge.

Research indicates that even when all I am doing is summarizing our disagreement, this is seen as a constructive act (and incidentally is something that experienced diplomats find themselves doing a lot).

Support and constructively challenge

Supportive behaviors aim at lessening stress and fear of failure, by encouraging, inviting challenge, exploring options, and coaching people for success. Supportive behaviors affirm and confirm. The results of supportive and challenging behaviors have been well documented and researched as the "Pygmalion effect":[3] people perform at the authority figure's level of expectation. If expectations are low they will rapidly notice, feel, "smell" this, and will deliver far less than they could. Show them you have absolute faith in their capacity to excel and they will do their best to prove you right.

A famous example is a US school experiment: Researchers pretended to have designed a reliable IQ test for children and asked teachers to volunteer to have their pupils tested. Some results of this fake test were then picked out at random and the researchers went back to the teachers, sharing with them (in confidence) the names of the "lucky few." Some teachers discovered with total surprise (you bet!) that kids who had not previously seemed well suited to academic life were, according to the test, very intelligent and with huge potential. The researchers left the teachers to bring out the hidden, unexploited potential in their classes and came back some months later. There was an interesting correlation between the results of the fake test and the new ranking of the pupils in class. Many of the kids (up to twice as many as in a control group) who had been labeled as having a high IQ were living up to that prediction. What had changed then? The test was not valid. The children were not supposed to be told about their results. The only people who knew were the teachers, who were also the only people who could have altered their behavior, attitude, and expectations towards the pupils. As the teachers changed their micro-behavior because of their revised expectations, the children started to improve their performance accordingly. (Simple things like giving these kids more attention than previously made a big contribution to the change.)

Companies' cultures are strongly influenced by the style of their leaders. Plot supportive and challenging behaviors on a grid, and see what happens. In which types of businesses would we find high challenge and low support behaviors (top left of the challenge/support matrix)? City of London and Wall Street firms? Consultancies? All these types of businesses, of which several are, ironically enough, called "partnerships"? What is the "smell" of such places? How does it feel to work there when you are at the top of your career, when you are a "rain maker"? Or when you made a mistake, when everybody avoids you, when a wall of silence and indifference tells you: "It is time to leave, loser."

Consider the types of activities found in the bottom-left box of the matrix (low/low). In our seminars, participants with experience of public administration often claim that it definitely falls into that category: no thrill, no fun. (Of course this reflects an outdated view of administration

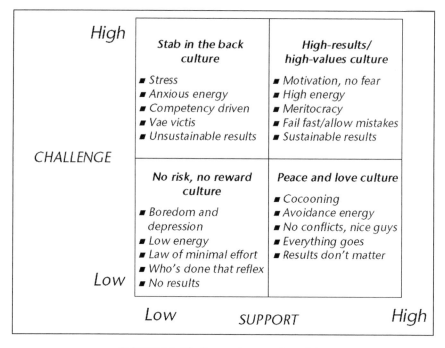

FIGURE 3.1 **Challenge/support matrix**

in some parts of the world.) What kinds of companies would be in the bottom-right corner (high support/low challenge)? Companies and organizations where the appearance of harmony is more important than the business itself, places where honest feedback and difficult discussions are avoided. Participants in our seminars sometimes suggest NGOs have that culture, which once again is a generalization but helps put a feeling on the culture.

The abundant post-mortem literature on Enron often refers to Ken Lay's convivial style of leadership. He is said to have avoided challenge in board discussions and one-to-one meetings alike, striving for harmony above all else. Unfortunately, this retreat from argument and challenge cut him off from realistic analysis of Enron's problems. Instead of building solid foundations for the harmony he cherished, he seemed to turn to heavenly support, trusting that "God will provide," with horrendous results. Enron's dream of "Endless Possibilities" became a nightmare for everyone because Lay personally sought only support and could not cope with challenge.

Reflect for a moment on where your company or team fits on the challenge/support matrix.

Clarify

"Are you all clear? Are there any questions in the room?" These are wonderful examples of unintentional value destruction through inappropriate closed questions. The leaders who ask them are convinced that they have briefed the troops about some new plan with all the clarity they intended. They are usually bitterly disappointed when actions and follow-up do not turn out as expected, and followers interpret their well-crafted plan in a completely unexpected manner.

Remember the sport which starts with a "T"? It is pretty much the same when we take clarity for granted. The sixth value-building behavior is about creating clarity (through listening, summarizing, and so on) and ensuring that, before the parties end the discussion, there is an intellectually compelling and emotionally binding contract between them.

"What is clear to you?" or "Before we leave I would like John to clarify what he thinks will happen next week" are much more useful clarifying questions.

Ask for time-out

There is an old story about the lumberjack who was so desperately behind with his work that he was trying to cut down trees with a blunt old saw instead of taking time to sharpen it. Some people prefer to talk about the "headless chicken syndrome." Too often, when a team is struggling, when the debate seems to have become sterile, people tend to switch their energy off and wait until the session is over (the passive attitude) or push their point harder (aggressive attitude). Rarely does someone propose a "time-out." If they did, they would be surprised at the smiles of gratitude on other participants' faces: "Finally someone is taking a stand here ... At last someone dares to say what we all thought: that this is going nowhere. Let's stand back and look at what is happening." Time-out means slowing down to enable the team or the process to speed up afterwards.

Time-out is about:

■ helping people step back from detail

- letting some heat out where necessary
- creating space to re-assert the big picture
- giving time to find out where everyone is in thinking and feeling
- focusing on questions such as: "What are we really here for? What are we doing here and now?"

Time-out works very well in basketball, ice hockey, or volleyball. It is built into the rules of the game, so that people can reflect on tactics and targets, and reframe the game so as to be and do their best.

Give feedback/run a review

The last of the eight value-building behaviors is about closure and learning. It is about reviewing the process of the discussion or the project ("post-mortem analysis") and understanding how each participant contributed to building value by their own styles and behaviors, or where they didn't and could have done better.

Feedback and review:

- show how/which behaviors facilitated or blocked success
- are the basis for continuous improvement
- allow praise or challenge of individual performance
- clear up misunderstandings
- build commitment to each others' development.

It is fascinating to observe the exponential increase in quality of the strategic dialogues of boards and executive teams when they adopt the discipline of review and feedback at the end of their weekly or monthly meetings. Those who do it rigorously find without exception that this behavior has a high pay-back. It is what the world's elite troops do in "after action reviews" or AARs. In that space of time, rank is ignored, a solid process review is undertaken, and each member of the team receives personal feedback intended to ensure shared learning so that the next mission comes as close to perfection as possible.

BEHAVIORS AND LEADERSHIP STYLES ARE CRITICAL IN VALUE CREATION AND DESTRUCTION

Can anyone seriously claim that strategies are the key competitive advantage in today's business battles? Strategies are a vital license to operate but are no longer a competitive advantage in today and tomor-row's knowledge economy and global, interlinked "flat world." The Holy Grail that companies are looking for is much deeper; it is about energy, passion, flexibility, adaptability, and similar qualities. No strategy can give you that as a stand-alone. Value creation is defined from the customer's perspective and all of these behaviors relate to the customer's satisfaction as well

Knowledge workers are the most sensitive type of people to deal with: if happy and satisfied, feeling recognized, respected, and significant, they will perform at their best. If upset, disappointed, depressed, or feel-ing insignificant, they will stop giving you that extra discretionary effort or knowledge and just do "what they are paid for." Knowledge workers react very strongly to the style of their leaders and co-workers. In fact the simplest form of sabotage is "I do not tell you what I know."

Part of the answer to these potential problems lies in the old but simply elegant situational leadership model of Paul Hersey and Ken Blanchard.[4]

Following that concept, leaders should adapt their style—telling, sell-ing, engaging (coaching in the original model) or enabling (delegating

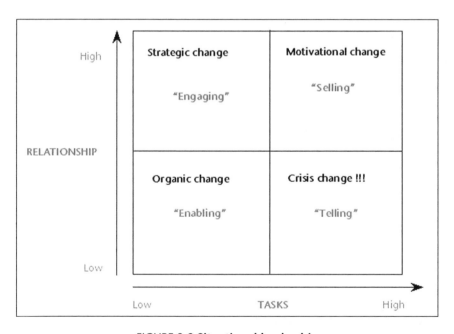

FIGURE 3.2 **Situational leadership**

in the original model)—to the situation. Two criteria should be considered: the urgency of the situation and the maturity of the followers in relation to that specific situation (maturity being determined by willingness and capability).

The situational leadership model identifies four styles of leadership. First is the "telling" style, the "my way or the highway" approach. This coercive, directive style is very appropriate in a crisis when followers have no idea about what to do to get out of it. The leader is expected to behave heroically and drive his troops across the sea to the Promised Land. Many celebrated heroes, from Moses to Sir Winston Churchill, have contributed to instilling in the collective unconscious the belief that leadership is about "Taking a courageous stand." This is the right attitude in times of crisis and threat, and it takes courage and sacrifice to do it. The downside of this style, particularly in the business context, is that it creates dependency on the hero (who is rapidly drawn into micro-management and, focusing on operational aspects, loses sight of wider concerns). It also can instill fear and distance, which is a terrible value destroyer, particularly when working with successful knowledge workers. Note that use of such a style suggests not only that there is a crisis situation (which is going to be more and more frequent in business) but also that the followers do not have the competences or intellectual ability to deal with it—but their leader does! Sending out such a message requires finely balanced consideration, particularly when surrounded by intelligent and gifted knowledge workers. "Telling" is the most appropriate style in times of crisis and change, when it appears that the subordinates have no clue about what to do or where to go next and expect the leader to take a clear, courageous stand.

The second style, "selling," becomes appropriate when the crisis is receding and followers start to regain confidence in their ability to deal with it. In educational terms, we are moving from early childhood (when constantly negotiating with a youngster is not recommended) towards adolescence, where more flexibility is required. Convincing and negotiating are among the leadership attributes here. However, the model still suggests that the leaders know best. They are encouraged to ask people to start thinking on their own and bring up propositions, but the final say remains with the leader because she knows better. The most obvious dangers here are being seen as manipulative ("Stop rhetorically asking for our opinions since you will decide what you want anyway!") and still "owning the truth" (therefore continuing to stifle the creativity and ownership of problems by others).

In our experience, over the last 20 years, these two styles (telling and selling) still dominate the leadership scene today, especially when leaders attempt to drive change. How many management conferences, conventions, "excoms," "excos," and the like see an audience PowerPointed to death in a succession of one-hour/one-way speeches by board members and experts, each followed by an unconvincing 15-minute Q&A session with questions carefully scripted by HR to avoid any of the leaders being put on the spot. This is archetypal over-selling, still with good intentions (lifting morale, reducing distance between the board and the next level) but achieving the opposite of what is desired. One of the authors sat through a recent choreographed meeting in Paris (1000 executives assembled three times in a week for two companies coming together: four hours of PowerPoint, 20 leaders on stage, and audience groans all around). All around, there were cynical comments. After 40 minutes rebellious comments started to surface from the rows and rows of executives, but they stayed in their seats. Ninety minutes later, the show was still going on and those on stage were oblivious to the mutiny in the audience—all they heard was the encouragement of the Press Relations executive who'd organized the event. The stage was playing to six national press journalists in the front row, not to the 1000 executives. When at last the meeting broke up, it was in an atmosphere of sarcasm and caustic "talking heads." The word *Guignol* (clown) was used repeatedly.

The third and fourth styles ("engaging" and "enabling") are less common, especially in times of uncertainty and change, even though they should be dominant. The engaging leader uses exploration and value-building behaviors as a way to engage people's intelligence and emotions behind the new vision.

The enabling leader is far from the *laissez-faire*, abdicating type sometimes described. This style is about creating conditions for people to do and be their best. In other words, ensuring that, through strategic clarity of purpose, development of appropriate competencies and strong motivation, the troops know what to do and therefore follow, or better still drive the business in, the right direction. "I must follow my people for I am their leader" the father of modern India, Mahatma Gandhi, used to say.

An interesting exercise demonstrating how such styles of leadership are better suited to the new converging environments than the more directive ones was brought back by one of our colleagues, Tony Page, from a seminar he had attended:

- Explain to the participants that they all have one individual objective: "To identify two people in the group and to go and stand at an equal distance between them." This seems like a pretty simple task at first glance. However, participants rapidly conclude it must be impossible (especially if there are 120 people taking part, as happened at INSEAD once): "If I choose x as a reference point and she chooses y who, in turn, has chosen me, it will be an endless vicious circle," everybody thinks.
- There are a few constraints:
  - Do not change the two reference people during the activity; they should always stay the same.
  - Stay on the agreed playing field (just to ensure people don't walk too far, which would simply delay the ending slightly).
  - No running (to avoid people colliding).
  - You must not show in any way who your two reference people are.
  - Do not try to organize this by talking. Any discussion relating to organizing this apparent mess is prohibited.

We've run this exercise, with groups ranging from ten to 250 people, more than a hundred times to date and it's always worked. In a maximum of three and a half minutes, the whole group comes to equilibrium and people have all reached their individual targets!

We follow up with a review on the appropriate style of leadership: How do you think an authoritative style would have solved this? In fact, we twice tried to run a parallel exercise with a designated leader, and twice had to stop after 15 frustrating (and unfair to the leader) minutes. After clearly explaining the task, the best leadership approach to such a complex issue is the "enabling" style where the leader (if any) gets out of the way and lets her team solve the problem.

CONCLUSION

Margaret Wheatley is a management consultant whose style and message leave no one indifferent.[5] Some people find great value in her unique and challenging ways of thinking while some others relegate her to the "New Age" type of dreamy but unrealistic preachers. We will let you make your own mind. In a challenging article on organizations and leadership, she asks: "Do leaders spend more time on policies and procedures to coerce people into Behavioral Change or do they try to engage their desire to contribute to a worthy purpose?"[6] And further on, she again asks change leaders where they put their energy:

- In selling the decision taken or involving people in the decision-making process?
- In solving the problem by themselves or figuring out how to involve people in the problem-solving process?

And she concludes: "While people are engaged in figuring out the future, they are simultaneously creating the conditions that facilitate more rapid and complete implementation."

Leaders are scrutinized by their people. The Hay Group, a consulting organization claimed that 70 percent of an organization's culture could be directly derived from the style of its leaders.[7] Engaging leaders are acutely aware of the impact of their behaviors on the organization and its people.

Behaviors create and destroy financial value every day in businesses. Using an inappropriate style of leadership in the wrong circumstances will "switch followers off" and they will withhold their discretionary effort, energy, and tacit knowledge. It is behavior rather than thought that destroys or creates value. Recurring micro-behaviors determine the boundaries of our social encounters, and those boundaries frame the social construction of reality.

CHAPTER 4

UNLEASHING POTENTIAL THROUGH THE EMOTIONAL AGENDA

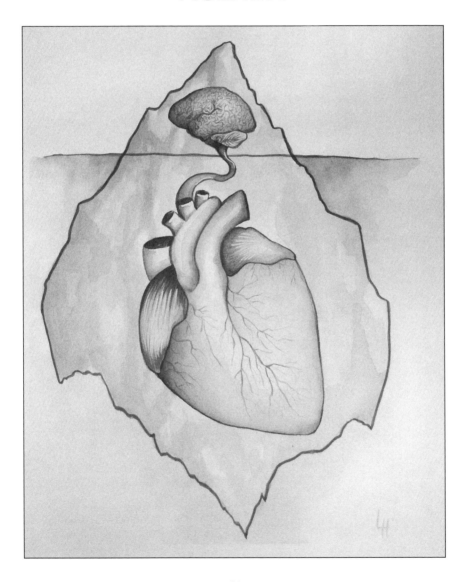

WHY A SENSE OF PURPOSE?

Few people better personify the notion of a sense of purpose and meaning than the Austrian neurologist and psychiatrist Viktor Frankl (1905–1997). Dr Frankl was of Jewish origin, but when the persecutions started under Nazi influence, followed by World War II, he decided to stay in Austria to support his patients. In 1942 he was arrested and deported to the concentration camp of Theresienstadt with his wife Tilly Grosser and both his parents. As a psychiatrist, Viktor Frankl was interested in what made some people want to live and survive at any cost, and what drove those who had suicidal tendencies (before the war he had treated thousands of women in the "suicide pavilion" of the General Hospital in Vienna).

Shortly before they were arrested by the Nazis, Tilly decided to hide the manuscript of her husband's writing on the sense of purpose in the lining of his jacket. The first day they arrived at the camp, the couple were separated, the manuscript was discovered, and the work of a whole life was sadistically destroyed in front of Viktor's eyes. His parents and then his wife died in different concentration camps, and Viktor himself passed through Auschwitz and Türkheim (near Dachau) before finally being freed.

As soon as he was liberated, he wrote a book in memory and reflection of his concentration camp experience called *Man's Search for Meaning* (trotzdem ja zum Leben sagen).[1] In this book, he explains how his theory (finding a meaning in every aspect of life) helped him survive the Holocaust. His manuscript had been destroyed as soon as he arrived in the camp? Then he would use his time there as an opportunity to test his theory against reality. Amongst the reports Frankl brought back from this journey to horror was the fact that inmates could always tell when one of them was going to die: that person would suddenly declare that there was no further reason to continue fighting for life, and soon afterwards would in fact be gone.

Dr Frankl's studies of his horrendous experience in the camps demonstrated that human beings need a strong sense of meaning (what we call a sense of purpose) to survive. He also added that "the psychologically healthy person chooses to do that which is absolutely determined for her," and urged people to stop wasting energy on fighting things that are going to happen anyway.

In 1998 the newly elected President of the American Psychological Association, Martin Seligman, challenged his peers to start looking at the bright side of life and understand what the happy people do to be, well, happy. The "psychology of happiness" (also called "positive psychology") was born.[2] Since then, that specialty area has been developing at high speed.

Workers in this field have established that two aspects are fundamental in explaining how ordinary people can be positive and happy on a sustainable basis. Those two aspects are directly applicable to business and leadership: living with a strong sense of purpose, and people's feeling that they have the capacity to influence their destinies.

HAVING A STRONG SENSE OF PURPOSE

Many of you will remember the story of the stone carvers that was widely quoted during the golden days of total quality management (TQM): it told how, in the Middle Ages, a man was walking through the site where a cathedral was being built. He was puzzled by the differences in energy, quality, and speed between the various stone carvers' teams. Being curious by nature, he went to three of the teams and asked their supervisors what they were doing. In the slowest and most disengaged team, the head replied, obviously surprised by the stupid question: "Well don't you see? We are carving stones here." The wise man then went to another team that seemed to be more animated; people were talking to each other, they were laughing and more energetic than the previous team. To his question, the reply was: "We are building a wall here." Finally he walked towards the head of the fastest-moving team. The feeling there was very different: everybody was doing something, each individual seemed to know what was expected, and like ants or ballet dancers all the people were moving and working in seamless coordination. When he asked the supervisor what he and his team were doing, the eyes of the man lit up and he beamed with a huge smile: "We are building the world's most beautiful cathedral!" The enquirer went away thoughtfully, wondering whether the difference in purpose could explain the difference in performance between the teams.

From our experience, we would reply a clear: Yes! There is a huge difference between doing a repetitively meaningless job (carving stones) and feeling one is contributing to an inspiring mission (building a cathedral). The story of the janitor at Cape Canaveral who, when President Kennedy asked what his job was, replied "I am sending a man on the moon" is equally illustrative.

Purposeful, reactive, or egocentric

A woman working for an important manufacturer of communication systems described a wearying management role:

> My challenge is to keep my team motivated. We are working on a product which is at the end of its life cycle. Another three years and it will be discontinued. My team is in charge of providing support to an ever-shrinking customer base. It is like tending to someone who is in the terminal phase of a mortal illness.

Our Dutch colleague Tritia, with her usual directness, asked her: "Then why did you take this job?" After an initial shock, the woman reflected for a few seconds then suddenly—and we could see the change in her— she was talking about her real purpose in the job: her eyes had recovered the light of hope, her tone was upbeat, and her whole body posture transmitted pride:

> Well the fact is, we are the future of this company. The few clients still using the old product would leave us forever if we suddenly abandoned our technical support for it. These clients will stay with us because we provide the best technical assistance, and they'll switch to our new technology because we've demonstrated our commitment to them on the old one. On top of that, I made it a personal battle to keep those 30 top engineers in the firm instead of seeing their jobs outsourced. They have the kind of knowledge I don't want our company to lose or share with competitors. That's what I am fighting for!

Her energy was back; she rediscovered her sense of purpose. When we are purposeful, we put energy behind our intentions!

When carefully observing teams and individuals alike, at work, playing sports, or even just having a simple conversation, three states are easily recognizable: purposeful, reactive, and egocentric.

The purposeful state

An individual in the purposeful state can be identified by the clarity she has about what she is doing, why she does it, and how this fits within her overall project (be it a minor goal or her "whole-life project"). Being clear about why she does things, that person projects a calm and determined resilience, as does a purposeful team. Such people are sure about themselves and are well prepared; when the unexpected happens, they review the actions to be taken in light of the purpose they follow. Their style of leadership is usually charismatic: being clear about what they want to achieve, they can usually describe it in an intellectually compelling and emotionally engaging way to their followers. An example is Aimé Jacquet, the legendary French coach of the national football squad that won the 1998 World Cup, talking to his team before the final against Brazil: "Tomorrow will be a feast, the best day of our lives."[3] Others include Henry V in Shakespeare's play, Sir Winston Churchill in his famous speech before the Battle of Britain ("We shall never surrender"), Gandhi, or Dr Martin Luther King ("I have a dream"). All are clear examples of leaders being in a purposeful state when inspiring their followers.

The reactive state

This state is sometimes confused with the previous one, because there is also quite a bit of energy here. However, the energy displayed is nervous, anxious—reacting against some threat. Purposefulness is about leading and shaping circumstances. The reactive state is about responding to and fighting circumstances. At a strategic level, firms which manage to maintain a "purposeful" strategy keep their competitors at arm's length and on their toes. They destroy or weaken the competition by keeping it reactive. Market leaders are constantly scrutinized by their competiters, and keep them wondering: "What will be their next move, what will they come up with?" Looking at market leadership with a next mover's perspective helps us predict who will be tomorrow's market leaders. When Apple came out with the I-phone, it was fascinating to look at the reaction of other phone makers. Those that were really sure about their core and purpose did take notice, did study Apple's innovation carefully, worked at understanding why it was such a success and what it meant for them, but displayed no anxiety. Rather they showed curiosity and willingness to learn and integrate the lessons in their own plans. Weaker competitors seemed to be in a state of panic, wondering "what's next?" The reactive state is necessary as a "wake-up call" but should be short lived. It is the reaction companies and individuals have when they move between the dream and Hell quadrants of the value matrix. This reactive state does not help a move back into the Heaven quadrant.

Toyota is the intellectual and market leader in the auto industry. It proclaims its purpose that "every driver should have the most enjoyable and safest drive," and the Toyota Business Processes System (TBS) maintains that purpose among the workforce. Toyota drives the industry.

The egocentric state

After drifting from the purposeful towards the reactive state, individuals and teams have two options: the reactive state can act as a wake-up call so that all their energies are invested into reactivating, recreating the purpose needed to achieve a purposeful state. Alternatively, abandoning the search for clarity and turning to a reactive posture, they drift further towards defensiveness and regression: the egocentric state. This is shown in cynicism, negative comments, blaming of circumstances and others for what happened. It can be a state of inaction but may also be frantic. Compensation and displacement behavior are substituted for purpose, and we do things for doing's sake not for purposeful results. When a company or a team is in this state, it usually demands that the leader first re-engage it through telling it what to do, since people need a solid dose of energy and purpose to get back into action. Paradoxically, however, egocentricity can be useful. My egocentric self is often the driver for my aspirational self: I do not want to be like that again so I will do something more positive.

WHAT IS THE SENSE OF PURPOSE?

So what is this sense of purpose which enables people and teams to become purposeful? The sense of purpose is emotionally connected, aspiring and inspiring, flexible and solid at the same time.

Emotionally connected

Kouzes and Posner in their book *The Leadership Challenge* invite us to try the following:[4] ask an audience what Paris means for them. The odds are that you will hear anything from "love, romance, restaurants, the Champs Elysées, the Eiffel tower" to "rude people, awful taxi drivers, and burned cars in suburban riots." How often will you hear a participant talk about the number of inhabitants, the city's geographical extent, the name of its mayor or other statistics? This is also Paris; however, people refer to an emotionally connecting image or memory first and *not* to intellectual data. We have run the "Kouzes & Posner test" hundreds of times and on every occasion their prediction has been fulfilled.

Aspiring and inspiring

If you wish to insult anyone in Nokia, tell them that they are in the mobile phone business. For Nokians, as they like to call themselves, their aim is truly "connecting people." Suppose that instead of this goal, their board had merely issued a technically descriptive mission statement. Can you imagine what the impact would have been on the future of that fast-moving and changing company? "Connecting people" means far more than producing a mobile phone: it is about sharing music, emails, web-browsers, taking pictures (how many would have predicted to the Nokia of the 1990s that the firm would become the world's biggest seller of digital cameras?) and sending them instantaneously. Nokia, which was producing footwear and car tires not so long ago, defines itself as an "internet company" nowadays.[5] How many companies are demotivating their people by unnecessarily long and descriptive visions or mission statements? "A home away from home," "We try harder," or "Making people happy" should be enough to let employees dream and take a stand on how to bring the vision to life. Years ago a friend of ours was complaining about the time he had to spend at the beginning of each winter season in training new staff at his hotel at Villars in the Swiss Alps. When we tried to understand what was so time consuming, he replied: "Well just imagine having to tell them where the knives, forks, and various types of spoons are, and this at the start of every season." We asked him: "Why don't you just transfer your passion? Why don't you make them proud of the long-established tradition of mountain hoteliers they are becoming a part of? New employees will soon find the spoons by themselves." Our friend tried this new purpose-based approach and has used it ever since.

- *Aspiring*: Many leaders hesitate to announce a grandiose vision for fear of failing to meet the expectations they raise. Stefan Stern's experience with the new laptop that we cited in Chapter 2 proves them right. However, as we pointed out in the Pygmalion principle, it is vital to provide people with a challenging target. People need a dream, something to reach out for. "Trying to be one of the best" isn't necessarily the most aspiring statement.
- *Inspiring*: Well-intentioned parents can disable their children by

being overprotective and over-caring. The same thing happens in business: well-meaning leaders tend to provide a plan, a vision, an aim which is too precisely described and discourages the followers by being too prescriptive and detailed. The sense of purpose aims at something superior and lets people create their own dream and their own way of engaging in it.

Flexible and solid

This concept relates to what is sometimes called "the essence." The essence is the simplest form of the purpose. It is flexible (therefore not too descriptive, but inspiring) and solid at the same time. Three non-business examples should make the point:

- French was once the language of business, aristocracy, and diplomacy, but has since lost out to English. Most people who have studied the matter relate this to a simple fact: The French have rigidified their language in a strictly coded manner (ferociously guarded by l'Académie Française) whereas English has remained a flexible, fast-evolving language with no academy to dictate the rules or ridicule non-native English speakers who attempt to express themselves in it. There are many kinds of English in the world but the most widely used is the non-codified "International English" where whatever one says is right as long as it helps the other party to understand what's been said. The essence of a language is to help communication between people. The language best adapted to that aim has taken over from the one that confused the procedure (coded language) with the purpose. A French lawyer acquaintance recently pointed out that one problem in French courts is that the subjunctive tense is used there as a mark of the elitist legal class; unfortunately, it confuses many of their clients who hardly ever use it.
- We ask your patience and understanding for the next example, where we talk in business terms about something that is sacred for many. The Catholic Church has been losing "market share" at an alarming rate in its "biggest market," Brazil. The biggest threat comes from the many smaller denominations, mainly from the United States: Baptists, Evangelists, and Adventists, among others. These newcomers on the Brazilian market have understood that the Catholic Church has drifted into a focus on rites and regulations far

69

removed from its essence (the divine, the sacred, the religious) and has been providing a very uninspiring message to the faithful for too long. To someone used to the traditional Catholic mass, it is a shock to take part in the service of another Christian denomination: People talk, sing, cry, laugh, dance, and applaud. This feels closer to real life, to real brotherhood—and closer to God. The late pope John Paul II had well understood that need for renovation and for a new fatherly relationship. His mass meetings (up to an amazing 5 million people in Italy) of young Christians were like nothing that had ever been seen before. The interesting thing is that when some of the young participants (who, in some cases, had rather liberal attitudes to "sex, drugs, and Rock'n'Roll") were asked why they were there, they often referred to the experience of finding a fatherly, sacred figure. John Paul II had well understood the need to go back to the essence and did a superb job in revitalizing the Roman Catholic Church (an effort apparently endangered by his more dogmatic successor). Some American (and Brazilian) Catholic churches have now added singing and clapping to their services to attract more people.

- A final, more festive example is about football. It is reported that, when Brazil won the world cup in 1994, one of the players was an adept of spiritualism and had convinced his teammates that, if they came onto the field holding hands in a human chain, the strength of all would be in each one of them (or maybe he was just a *Stars Wars* aficionado). The images of the team coming onto the pitch for each game seemed to reflect that belief. In 1998, during the next World Cup, the coach went for the process instead of trying to understand the essence: He told the players to enter the stadium holding each others' hands, without explaining the purpose. The pictures of the 1998 squad entering the stadium showed the evident embarrassment of the poor players at coming onto the pitch like kindergarten children told to hold hands with each other without understanding why.

A sense of purpose must therefore take into account the essence, the "why," while preparing to question all the procedures and processes around it.

THE CAPACITY TO INFLUENCE

Benjamin Franklin is quoted as wisely saying: "Tell me and I will forget. Teach me and I will remember. Involve me and I will learn."

A massacre in the United States on 2 October 2006 was instantly depicted in vivid detail by media throughout the world. One of the neighbors of an Amish community had gone mad and, in a desperate killing spree, had raided the Amish school and killed five little girls between seven and 13 years old. Even the courageous sacrifice of Marian Fisher, 13 years old and the oldest child in the group, who asked the man to kill her and let her friends go, didn't calm his madness. The young girl was shot first, then nine others, and when the police finally stormed the school, the man had also killed himself.

The story is horrible and has depressed the whole world. Much less widely known is the way the Amish community reacted towards the widow and children of their daughters' killer. Some of the Amish relatives of the dead or wounded children went instantly to the widow and orphans in order to support and console them; some of them went to the killer's funeral to support his family and even collect money for them. The widow of the murderer spoke in tears in front of the TV cameras about the unbelievable support she was getting from the Amish Community.

How does this terrible event relate to the capacity to influence and the psychology of happiness? It is very revealing to reflect on the reaction of the Amish parents. Why did they forgive their daughter's assassin?

The few experts who were asked suggested that this was part of the Amish religion and belief.[6] Many, rightly, found remarkable this "walking the talk" of their faith by those no less remarkable people. It wouldn't be an unreasonable assumption to believe that, should they be asked, the members of the community would probably explain this amazing reaction in much the same way.

There was however, another complementary human response taking place, one that it is extraordinary and unusual: When your daughter has been killed in an atrocious way, what can you hope for? What in life can you hope to influence when your beloved child is under your eyes in the coffin? The Amish still had the power to greatly influence the life of an innocent widow and devastated orphans. They could have chosen to make the family's mourning hidden, shameful, and secret; they could have condemned them to live forever with a name dirtied for eternity and the dreadful memory of a girls' killer as a father and husband; they could have marked those children and this woman with a red brand for the rest of their lives ... or they could, in accordance with their faith, support the widow and the orphans and actively forgive them.

The simple fact of having the choice, however dreadful it might be, must have greatly supported the Amish families in their own mourning process and given some kind of meaning to the slaughter and sacrifice of five innocent young girls.

Stephen Covey wrote about the circles of influence in his famous book *The Seven Habits of Highly Effective People.*[7] We have reworked these in the light of work done on purpose and influence, and the three circles that we work with are those of control, of influence, and of doom.

The circle of control

Here, a person has or is expected to have full control over things. In the workplace, this circle is clearly identified in a job description for example.

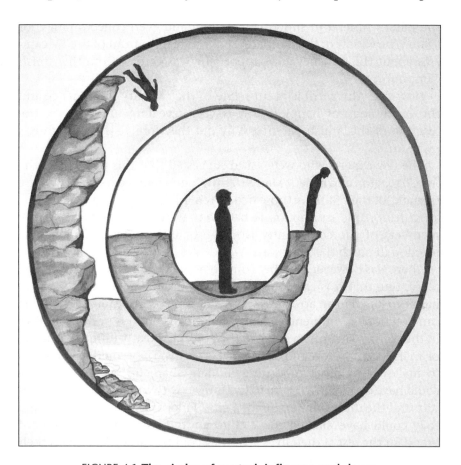

FIGURE 4.1 **The circles of control, influence and doom**

Problems arise when someone refuses to take a stand, ownership, initiative, or action on the prescribed items. An often forgotten dimension of this circle is that it also is your "license to operate." Effectiveness in this area is what others expect from you. Forget trying to exercise influence (the next circle) if you are not perceived as "having done your homework": That is, as having delivered on what is inside your control zone.

The circle of influence

This is the gray area. It is unclear whether or not one has authority here, whether one is allowed to operate in this zone. However, wanting to extend one's circle of influence is a sign of well-being, of willingness to grow, of having a strong sense of purpose. People are expected to enter this zone once they have proved themselves in the previous circle of control. Others will, likewise, invite a person to enlarge her circle of influence once she has been perceived as excelling in the circle of control.

The circle of doom

The circle of doom is the "dark side." When people are here, all they see are amplified negatives. When someone is in this zone, you will hear blame, accusations, "me against the system," "I could if they'd listen to me" types of complaints. It is the zone of "bitching and moaning" and could also be relabeled "the loser's corner." The interesting thing is: how does one fall into that circle? Usually, people find themselves there when they are trying to influence things and people but have failed to demonstrate credibility in the control circle. They think they are in the influence circle when others don't. The others refuse to be influenced by people who have no credibility, and those who try to exert influence become increasingly frustrated at not being listened to, not being capable of influencing. Stay in the zone of doom long enough and you will develop a "negative fantasy," which is a defensive routine: "I know I should have done something but if I had it would have been the end of the world we know, so I will not do anything." Statements like this are a defensive attempt to justify someone's failure to do anything purposeful.

A recent individual example might help understand the process of influence and the loss of influence. Most of us are engaged in not-for-profit activities, in parallel with our commercial practice. In that context, one of our partners is coaching staff in a school which has great educational ideals. She was asked by the Principal to explore what was happening to a recently hired nurse who had become, against all expectations, very bitter and demotivated. She sought her out at lunch and listened to her story.

The nurse had previously had a very successful career as a specialist in child/adolescent care, which was why the school had hired her. In their approach, well-intentioned HR people had painted a rosy picture, especially of one aspect where the nurse, like any human being, was keen to use her energy: influence! She had been promised (or at least this is what she had understood) that she would be very influential in the school's health policy, which was also an open door to influencing school strategy and overall operations. It is hard to be sure what she was really told, and what her ear selectively chose to hear and capture. In short, however, our nurse dreamed of quickly becoming the unofficial number two, a key influencer to the Principal, and that was the basic expectation with which she took up her new position. Needless to say, the unfortunate lady was rapidly disillusioned and "brought back to Earth." Her response to these initial rebuffs was to try harder, to listen less, and push her points of view more strongly. In turn, the community became equally uncompromising, not to say harsher. By the time she had lunch with our colleague, she was bitterly disappointed and looking for a new job. It seemed a great loss for both sides.

After listening and letting her blow off steam, our partner asked the nurse to assess how well she had tried to build herself a "license to operate" by proving she was the brilliant nurse she had been hired as. To her surprise, she realized that she had been too busy "politicking her way up," that she had, indeed, neglected the work she was primarily there to do. This recognition was a first indication of growing awareness. She had tried to jump too fast and too far, and the organization was pushing back, expecting her to prove herself first.

Luckily for her (though sad that it had to happen), shortly after that meeting a young girl became deeply depressed and threatened to commit suicide. Our nurse, called in the middle of night to a scene of emotional turmoil, found herself back in her control zone. In a highly professional and caring manner she managed to reason with the adolescent, bringing her back to her room and getting her off to a deep, quiet sleep after a long and helpful talk. Everybody was flabbergasted and lost in admiration, including the Principal, who felt he was seeing her almost for the first time. He invited her to discuss the situation the next day, and her influence rapidly grew inside the school.

This story demonstrates how people can get lost in the circle of doom because they have not earned their license to influence from the people around them. You win your license by first showing competence in your control zone.

Going back to the horrendous story of the Amish people, the parents of the young victims could have easily fallen into the circle of doom ("My God why us? Why did you let this happen?") if their faith hadn't helped them regain control and influence on their environment by deciding to forgive and actively support the widow and orphans of their daughters' killer.

That is how powerful and necessary the capacity to influence is in human beings. The need to influence, when used positively, supports a sustainable emotional agenda. It is reflected in our need to feel significant when we lack influence: the insignificance experienced becomes the main reason for something most leaders would like to understand how to fight: Resistance to change.

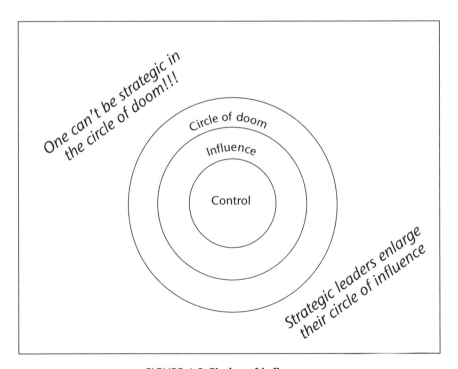

FIGURE 4.2 **Circles of influence**

KILLING THE FEAR (FLOURISHING, NOT LANGUISHING)

For 180 million Brazilians, 12 July will remain a day of national mourning after their team (the famous "Seleção") fell victims to a daring and enterprising French team in the final of the 1998 Football World Cup.

Most neutral observers (and Didier was far from being able to claim to be neutral, dressed head to toe in the green and yellow colors of Brazil as he watched the final at the Parkers' home in Switzerland) were shocked by the contrast between the two teams: a daring, risk-taking, fearless French team practicing "champagne football" annihilated a terrified, doom-laden, uninventive, and boring-to-watch Brazilian squad.

Before the final, Didier had sent Brazil's biggest daily paper an article called "Why Brazil will lose the World Cup," which was never published. It discussed the counterproductive impact of using fear and emotional blackmail to motivate the players. Weeks after the lost final, he was explaining why the leadership style of the Brazilian coach was amongst the causes of the defeat when a participant challenged him to understand instead why the French won. So he went searching ...

The conclusions were fascinating: in terms of "strategic agendas" the two teams had comparable strategies and tactics, while in terms of individual abilities the Brazilians were far superior, with five of their team in the list of the world's ten best players. The most noticeable difference was in the style of the coaches and their underlying belief systems.

Both coaches had high reputations. Mario Zagalo of Brazil is the only man in the world to have won the cup as a player (1958), as team captain (1962), as coach (1970), and as assistant coach (1994). However there was one critical difference between the highly-capped Zagalo and the comparatively unknown French coach Aimé Jacquet: the latter was determined to "kill the fear" whereas his Brazilian counterpart seemed to use it, with good intentions, believing it would serve as a powerful motivator. The results were blatantly obvious on the pitch: a liberated French team, daring and full of ardor, whose members, as the coach put it, were either "busy taking a personal risk or busy supporting someone else who was busy taking a risk,"[8] and a petrified Brazilian team where it seemed that no one was willing to take a risk and be subsequently blamed for a mistake.

Seeking to discover whether there was any scientific reason for this, Didier was introduced by Jacques Fradin, a French medical doctor and founder of the Institut de Médecine Environnementale, to the thinking and work of the famous French biologist and philosopher Henri Laborit.[9] In conjunction with the work of Paul McLean and D. Goleman[10] ("emotional hijack"), this throws a fascinating light onto the result of fear on humans. Building on Dr McLean's triune brain concept (this has recently been disputed on the grounds that reptiles also have a cortex), one can simplify the way the three main parts of the brain (analyzed from a fear/stress standpoint) react to fear and aggression.

The reptilian brain

Constantly, 24 hours a day, our reptilian brain scrutinizes the environment around us, testing the "threat level." This part of the brain is what we have in common with other animals and is very instinctive. It is the "historical" brain in humans. On its battlements are three red flags ready to be waved:

- *Survival threats*: In prehistoric days, the capacity to detect and respond to threats made the difference between life and death, between the survival of a species or tribe and its disappearance from Earth. This faculty has survived throughout our evolution and been transferred from *homo erectus* to *homo officius* (the one whose habitat is office space). In today's terms, fear for survival is triggered when the management consultants walk in and the executives start to talk about rationalization and cost cutting. Fear for survival is fear of losing our job in today's working environment.
- *Territorial threats*: As we still see with many animals, control of territory is a critical component of well-being. For our ancestors too, territorial threats meant the danger of a poorer land in terms of hunting, feeding, drinking, protection, and other necessities. The territory was the trademark of the tribe. In today's corporate terms, the territory represents everything attached to prestige, ego, and self-image: from the size of my department, the hierarchical level I operate to, the visibility I have with the board, down to my private parking space and the many small (and big) perks the firm offers. Being entitled to them increases my self-esteem; being stripped of them makes me feel like the wretched Alfred Dreyfus when he was unjustly degraded from his army rank and imprisoned for a crime he never committed.[11] Threatening people's status is a powerful activator of the fear red flag in the reptilian brain.
- *Habit threats*: From prehistoric times to the present day, threatening people's habits has been a sure way to trigger their fear and related defense mechanisms.

The limbic brain

As soon as our "fear flags" have been activated, a message is sent to our limbic brain asking it to develop an appropriate response, most commonly known as a "defense mechanism." To simplify, amongst the many reflexes that humans have developed, the main three are known as the "three F's" (a fourth one exists but we would never be published under the neo-Puritan US government, if we were to elaborate on it):

- *Fight*: This is an obvious defense response. Fighting is not necessarily physical; it can also be verbal, cynical, defeatist, ironic, or take other forms. The good thing for a leader though is that when followers fight (against change for example) they tell you openly that your plans have inspired fear.
- *Flight*: It is much more difficult to spot this response. It is about avoidance, pretending to be on board, playing the game when in fact the person has switched off and is already looking for a job elsewhere while you continue paying their salary.
- *Freeze*: This is the most damaging of the three to the individual. In his research with rats, Laborit found that those who couldn't fight or fly were liable to develop pathologic illnesses. Inhibition is a defense mechanism but very damaging to its user.

The limbic brain is therefore the center of reactions to perceived threat and fear. Other than launching a defensive move, as Goleman explains, it also produces a hormone, cortisol, which has an amazing capacity: it switches off and temporarily isolates another part of the brain called the neo-cortex.

The neo-cortex

This is the center of creativity, adaptation, logic, and entrepreneurship. It is the very part of the brain that consultants, executives, and leaders of all sorts call upon when they bravely announce tremendous changes, but the style they often adopt can push their followers to shut down the neo-cortex and disconnect it from the rest of the brain. There is of course a historical explanation of why our brain reacts in this way to fear or danger: back in the old days, when a threatening grizzly was heading their way, it wouldn't have been very wise for our ancestors to sit back and conceptualize about the danger. Their reptilian brain would immediately signal the threat to their limbic brain, which would switch off the reflective brain (neo-cortex) and engage in fight, flight, or freeze as the most appropriate response.

Our brain was (and still is in certain situations) amazingly well adapted to our survival. The problem is that it reacts in the same old way in the corporate context. Trigger fear, justified or not, inside people and, far from unleashing their fullest potential, you will drive them towards minimal risk taking, unquestioning obedience, and a "cover my ass" attitude. Consider how many well-intentioned leaders have attempted to motivate their followers but have in fact disabled them completely through inappropriate triggering of fear.

People appreciate being given the potentially frightening news, the hard facts, but they do not appreciate being frightened in the process.

The recurring fears

One measure of normality in human beings is the desire to be part of society. The desire to be included is a natural human need; psychopaths do not display the empathy for others implicit in this need. A basic fear in normal people is the fear of rejection, particularly rejection by valued role models. "If I say that to him, he won't invite me to the next meeting" is an internal warning that many people feel. The fear of rejection is stronger than actual rejection. People invest a lot of time in achieving and sustaining inclusion, and will engage in many forms of compensation and avoidance behavior in order to remain included.

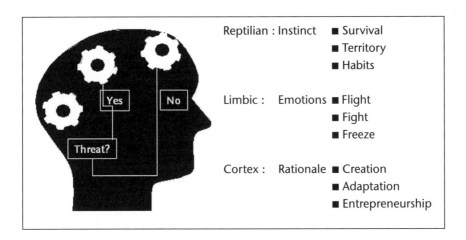

FIGURE 4.3 **Three brains**

79

The fear of incompetence will stop people taking risks, experimenting, and admitting mistakes. Everyone feels incompetent at times in situations of change, but in a psychologically safe environment people will overcome this fear and take the risk of experimenting and learning. The underlying drive is for control, the need to stay in control of your capacity to act in any situation. Leaders play a critical role in helping people enhance their sense of control of issues and in displaying behaviors that create a safe emotional space.

The fear of betrayal or abuse of trust will stop people from being open about issues, concerns, and personal values and positions. When people have this fear they tend to hold back, be tentative with information and their intuitions. Openness, trust, and intimacy create deep bonds that can carry people through very challenging times. Leaders can help overcome fears by being vulnerable themselves, sharing concerns without frightening people, and also showing humility. Arrogance and macho behavior will block openness and intimacy to the detriment of shared identity, creativity, and the sense of mutual support.

Inclusion, control, and openness issues lie behind 80–90 percent of the difficult emotional moments and hidden agendas in business. Working with empathic questions to bring out these concerns can save a lot of wasted energy. People press for organization changes in order to get more inclusion, when maybe more face-to-face meetings with colleagues might achieve it more easily. Managers block team projects for fear of losing control, others refuse to collaborate for fear that their openness will be abused. If we dig to find the core issues in an organization, they will be located in one or more of these three emotional spaces.

Stretch versus stress

We are often challenged in seminars and public speeches by participants who claim that "sometimes fear is good because it gives us a solid kick in the ass and forces us forward," and who go on to provide a good list of examples that range from succeeding at exams to saving life in dramatic situations. The confusion here is between stress (which we have described as counterproductive) and stretch, which is related to the "raising the bar/rising to the occasion" that we covered when talking about the Pygmalion effect. Stretching people is good: it is about challenging them, encouraging them, convincing them they "can do it." That is sensible leadership practice. Doing it in a supportive, enabling way usually produces good results. Threatening people, instilling fear, suggesting that "if they don't succeed then ..." will push them into the defensive mode and all the phenomena we described above. The work quoted earlier, *Bad is Stronger than Good*, confirms that this applies across many psychological fields: if we trigger fear it will be the fear response that is conditioned, not the solution to the problem. Some leaders generate fear in others to make themselves feel good, but it destroys learning capabilities and creativity. Fear does not create a psychological space that is safe and, as Marcial Losada points out, when groups are frightened their behavior changes to a languishing state, where fixated discussions circle around the threatened point, hopelessness sets in, and people start to focus on negative internal dynamics rather than external factors which may be the road to salvation.

This response, however, provides us with a great bridge towards another eye-opening model derived from the work and research of Australian psychologist Michael Apter, who in the mid-1970s presented (with his colleague K. C. P. Smith) the "reversal theory," according to which "motives and emotions change, depending on the meaning a person attributes to a particular situation."[12] Combining this with our observations of sports and professional teams at work, we developed the "energy model," which has several links to emotion and performance.

THE ENERGY MODEL

The energy model looks at four distinctive psychological states: Relaxation, which is contrasted with anxiety, and excitement, set in counterpoise to boredom. People and teams alike switch rapidly between these states, flipping temporarily into four dramatically different zones of energy or emotional space: Performance, stress, depression, and "the parking zone" (Figure 4.4). How does this work?

The performance zone (or purposeful state)

The performance zone is comparable to the purposeful state described earlier. This means that, as a leader, you manage to keep your team in a relaxed state. That doesn't mean laziness, contentment or complacency; it is about:

■ having created (co-created) a shared and clear sense of purpose (Why are we here, how will this fit in the bigger picture when we have succeeded?)

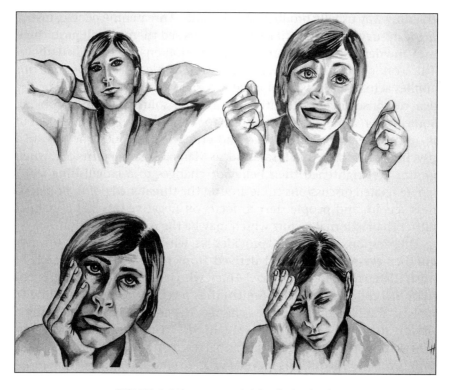

FIGURE 4.4 **Energy model (artistic view)**

- having ensured all team members feel confident in their ability to get the work done
- ensuring team members have a sense of pride, satisfaction about what they do, and the competence to do it.

It is also about getting the team excited by what they do, "putting them in flow" by having:

- created a motivation for what they do
- enabled them to feel they can achieve it (a can-do attitude)
- transmitted a clear sense that they can be successful.

When teams and individuals are at the same time relaxed and excited, they find themselves in the performance zone. Athletes call this "the zone." People in the zone have confidence that they can succeed and the passion to reach their objective. This was clearly the case for the French team when they entered the Stade de France for their final against Brazil on 12 July 1998. The players were relaxed, their coach having done a superb job in managing anxieties, showing faith and the belief his team would win, and depicted a sufficiently clear, attainable, and credible picture of what would victory look like once they had beaten Brazil. (We guess he didn't have much to do to create the motivation for—to excite—professional players to get ready for the challenge of playing the final against the world's reputed best team.)

The stress zone (or reactive state)

The stress zone is the equivalent of the reactive state. This is where the Brazilian team was. Like the previously mentioned individuals and teams, people in the stress zone are excited and motivated but their relaxed state has changed into something anxious, nervous, or reactive. Fear, stress, and rigidity are the trademarks of the anxious state. In the stress zone, the energy is very reactive, with lots of nervous running around (headless chicken syndrome), and the defense mechanisms are ready to roll. There is a lot of activity that is not necessarily used in the most effective way.

The depression zone (or egocentric state)

Entering the depression zone is very much like drifting from the reactive state to the egocentric one. Teams and individuals falling into the depression zone are anxious (they know they should do something about it) and helpless (too weak, too bored, too disengaged to do so). It is a victimization state, in which cynicism, negativism, and depression are displayed. The Brazilian team certainly fell into that state after the defeat, with their coach trying to point the finger and find scapegoats for the failure (except himself of course).

The parking zone (or neutral state)

Despite its name, the parking zone is probably one of the most interesting zones to study: it is sometimes a positive place to be (when it is used as a space for recovery, reflection, and recreation) sometimes negative (when it drifts into disengagement and neutrality). Someone in this zone is at the same time relaxed (no threats, no anxiety, and no fear) and bored in the sense of either being explicitly bored (as when I talk too much) or dozing and temporarily switched-off. That state allows people to re-invent themselves, reassess a situation or opinion, and take a stand. They are in a kind of daydream, preparing themselves to switch towards performance, stress, or depression.

The levers of the energy model

So, as a leader, what are the levers you can pull in order to keep yourself and your team as much as possible in the performance or parking zones?

How do we bring a person or a team from boredom towards excitement? Passion, motivation, raising the bar, awareness, encouragement are factors that will probably come to mind. Getting back to the value-building behaviors, this all could be clustered as the "challenge" behavior. Likewise, moving people from anxiety to relaxation will happen with support behavior.

Challenge and support are the two levers of the energy model that we work with, and which the victorious French coach Aimé Jacquet consciously used in his leadership style to bring his "boys" to the top of the planet Football.

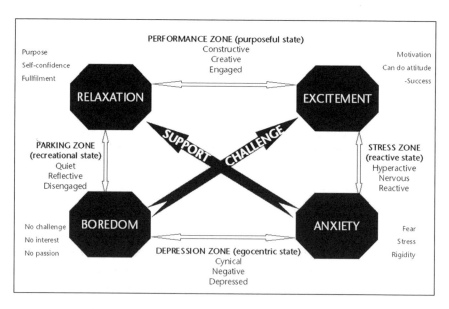

FIGURE 4.5 **Energy model (inspired by M. Apter)**

CONCLUSION

Take the analogy of an automobile: If we want to run the car properly there are system components that we need to use in parallel to be effective. The strategic/intellectual agenda is like the GPS of the car. Without a solid intellectual agenda, people might expend their energy in vain. No one wants to join a project, a team, or a leader that can't express clearly what they want. The famous French author Molière used to say: "What is conceivable clearly can be expressed clearly." Co-creating clarity on the intellectual agenda is the start of the journey. It should be undertaken at the earliest possible moment as a collective exercise.

The behavioral agenda is the body of the car: It is what people see from the outside (behaviors make the brand) and what people feel on the inside (the "smell of the place"). Behaviors create value (when they help the project forward) or destroy it (when they block people, energy, or clarity).

Finally, the emotional agenda is the fuel of the engine. Without it, we might know through the GPS where we want to go (strategic intent), we might have a great leadership culture and friendly behaviors, but lack the passion to move, the willingness to take risks, fail, and learn. Then nothing happens and the strategy remains an illusion.

CHAPTER 5

ACCELERATING CHANGE: THE LEADERSHIP ENGAGEMENT PROCESS

THE LEADERSHIP ENGAGEMENT PROCESS: EVERY WORD COUNTS

- *Leadership*: If leaders are not fully committed, ready to open up their defenses and take personal risks, willing to reduce the distance between them and their troops, prepared to build intimacy, able to show vulnerability and admit temporary incompetence, an engagement process is illusory. You cannot separate strategy from leadership; they have to be intimately connected in the individual leader.
- *Engagement*: We like to talk about the "intellectually compelling"— that is, what is rationally convincing—and about the "emotionally engaging": what will rouse people from indifference and put energy into their intentions.
- *Process*: Engagement can't be built on mere responses to events; it has to be built into a longer-term and purposeful agenda.

It is worth putting energy into the leadership engagement process and skill set. It is an effective way to successfully implement sustainable change. It helps remove the barriers to change and engages people in the new strategic, organizational, or cultural direction. It works through the three agendas discussed in Chapter 1.

A word of warning: Leadership engagement is not a panacea! Keeping in mind the old and robust situational leadership model, one could say that there are several ways to bring change about and handle the necessary communication:

- *The one-man show*: This is the equivalent of the "telling" style. It is the right type of engagement when there is a crisis, when no discussions can be allowed and when a rapid wake-up call is needed. It is easy to remember such meetings. Who hasn't seen the "roaring" Steve Balmer,[1] just after he was appointed CEO of Microsoft, screaming (a bit out of breath) and with a killer's look in the eyes: "I LOVE THISS COMPANEYY, YEAHHH!"[1] Not really wise for a participant to ask for clarity, seek to explore, or share his doubts in such circumstances.

    The "one-man show" style of engagement means one-way communication too: Slides, video, light and laser shows. This type of engagement meeting can be appropriate when morale has to be boosted and the leaders are expected to show fierce resolve and the way forward. The downside is that questions remain unasked and people have no time to either explore or test the way proposals might apply in their field.

■ *The listen-to-me show*: Most of the yearly meetings, conventions, and gatherings that we see follow this model, associated with the "selling" style. Top management gets up on stage and seeks to convince with PowerPoints and slideshows. A few moments are allowed for the traditional Q&A sessions, but usually participants know what to ask and what not to ask. The style is different from the previous one (sounding more amicable, intellectual, and cozy) but the process is pretty much the same: One-way delivery—We are not really interested in what you think, please listen, understand, and cascade down. This style is, however, a good alternative in cases of emergency and challenges for which the audience is unprepared.

■ *The leadership engagement process* is fundamentally different. The style can be strong and energetic or softer. It still needs some inspiration, from a customer perhaps rather than a leader, but the message is different:

  – We are here to co-create, not to passively sit down and consume.
  – We are interested in your questions and concerns, as well as in your creativity and ideas.
  – Our style will match our message.
  – We need your total engagement, not just blind obedience.

THE EIGHT MISCONCEPTIONS ABOUT THE LEADERSHIP ENGAGEMENT PROCESS

We will never forget look of shock, almost terror, on the face of a board member's personal assistant: "Leadership engagement? With the 300 top leaders of our company? Unthinkable! We can't involve people in setting the strategy. It would be too dangerous ..." That organization was eventually taken over after repeatedly failing to engage its employees in the frenzy of change that its board drove forward.

Too often, leaders believe that strategy has to be a secretive process and that they "can't ask so many people what they think the strategy should be." Let us look at the eight most common misconceptions about co-creation of clarity:

■ *People would want to redesign the strategy*: Wrong! Our numerous engagement workshops, ranging from 20 to several hundred participants, all, without exception, demonstrated that participants neither want nor feel the need to be deeply involved in designing and implementing the new strategy. Bankers want to remain bankers, chemical engineers want to work in their plants, and designers are longing to get back to the drawing board ... People expect their boards to do the governance work which is in their control zone, and are happy to let them do so. They expect board members to have done their homework, with or without consultants. Whenever audiences are asked to participate in designing a strategy, the silence is deafening. So what *do* people want? They want to be given time, space, and authorization to explore, challenge, understand what the management asks them to engage in. They want to be able to question and summarize the new strategy before fully committing themselves to it. That does not mean they want to create it!

■ *People don't have enough strategic knowledge; we will be wasting our time in pointless discussions*: Wrong! In a research study frequently attributed to the Dale Carnegie training organization, the top 500 firms in the United States were asked about the levels of the hierarchy which had produced the ideas that had transformed their business in the last 20 years. Between 3 and 5 percent of the initiatives that revolutionized businesses were reported to originate from senior management, slightly less than a third were from middle management, and approximately two-thirds came from "operational people." Of course the law of numbers grossly skewed the data (there are many more people at the base than at the top) but still that is where the best ideas were coming from. Co-creating clarity is never a waste of time. Great ideas about implementing the strategy flourish in such large audiences.

■ *People will be negative*: Wrong! Our experience in the many engagement processes we ran was always the opposite. Yes, people may be cynical, skeptical, or suspicious at the start of the process. They are, above all, a bit ill at ease to gather in such large numbers in an unfamiliar environment where they quickly realize there will be no place to hide, no room for passengers. Yet the first sessions of the process almost always end up on a high, with people grateful and appreciative of the risk taken by their leaders and the openness and trust they have demonstrated.

■ *People will say that it is our job to set strategy*: Wrong! That attitude ("The board should know ... Why are they asking us?") is sometimes encountered. It is however a minority view and people who hold it don't keep it for long; they are persuaded into a more responsible attitude by the strong and positive peer pressure which develops through the process. In fact this concern is far more widespread amongst leaders who still

91

believe that it is their job to know, that they should come with a solution (back to the telling/selling assumptions and functioning modes) than it is among their followers.

- *We shouldn't scare them by saying ...*: Wrong! Many well-intentioned executives are concerned about being "too open" in their encounters with their employees. They fear they might create a wind of panic, a wave of negativity, or might trigger rumors when they are just attempting to explore new possibilities. Clarity is their concern. That is our concern as well, and when kicking a leadership engagement process off, leaders have to be clear. They must not hesitate to state— several times if necessary—what is "cast in stone" and what is open for discussion (and to what extent), what is proposed for exploration and what is simply a management communication on which no comments are required.

- *We can't tell them everything*: Wrong! Just after Ron Teerlink was appointed to the board of ABN-Amro, he was about to speak to the top 250 people in the operations department. Out of the blue, he was told that rumors of imminent lay-offs were running around the company. Ron didn't shy away from the discussion. He simply told the audience:

  > There are three types of questions I expect you will ask me: questions to which I know the answer, and I will respond to them straightaway. There will also be questions—which I expect to be a majority—to which I don't know the answer, and we should think about these together. Finally there will be those for which I have an answer but one I cannot give publicly now, either because respecting confidentiality is the CEO's privilege, or because people concerned haven't been spoken to yet.

  As you might expect, most of the questions asked were thrown back at the audience, some were answered on the spot, and for three (three only) he had to "play his joker"—and the participants all understood and respected this. In fact, nature abhors a vacuum. The no-comment responses will trigger far more comment, speculation, and rumor than if things have been laid out correctly and clearly. Where facts are withheld, rumors will always spread out of proportion and with a theatrical exaggeration that could have been avoided if leaders had the courage to come and engage with their troops.

- *The employees will disagree amongst themselves*: Right! And so what? The purpose of the process is to create debate and explorations. People will not necessarily agree immediately, and that is a sign of engagement. However, we have never, ever had internal disagreements that have blocked and crippled the whole process. In fact there is a deliberate technique we use (learned from Richard Pascale) called "Valentines," where we make sure we bring out disagreements among functions and regions: at an early stage we ask the different groups to give their perceptions of each other and challenge tacit assumptions.

■ *We will be exposed*: Right! And is it better to stay hidden on the 30th floor behind a phalanx of secretaries and PAs? When change happens, leaders are expected to show the way, be role models for their people. If we were talking to a "Texas cowboy" kind of audience, we would stress that leadership engagement is not for the "faint at heart," but this is not the point. The exposure leaders get is a positive one. "Courageous vulnerability" is a leadership skill that has massive impact, as a vivid example shows. "You can't change? Let me show you!": two pictures came up on the screen, one of the CEO (who was right there on stage and challenging his troops) when he was 30 kilos overweight, and one of him much slimmer and fitter. The courageous Fieke Sijbesma, Chairman of Royal DSM, pointed out that this change had involved a 36-month process with doubts and pain everyday.

THE THREE STEPS IN A LEADERSHIP ENGAGEMENT PROCESS

How many books have been written on change, and how few take into consideration the psychological aspect of it? Change leadership is not a mechanical, project-based process (that is better called change management). It takes into account the three dimensions of *logos* (intellectual/strategic agenda), *ethos* (behavioral agenda), and *pathos* (emotional agenda).

Our approach is based on three steps, as shown in Figure 5.1. This matrix shows on the vertical axis a simple positive–negative emotional range, and on the horizontal axis the three psychological stages of egocentrism, reactivity, and purposefulness.

The three steps are therefore:

■ *The mourning process*: Negative emotions (the change has been imposed on us) and the egocentric/depressed state where people tend to close down. Recovery through catharsis is what leaders must seek in this step, and we will see later how to proceed with this.

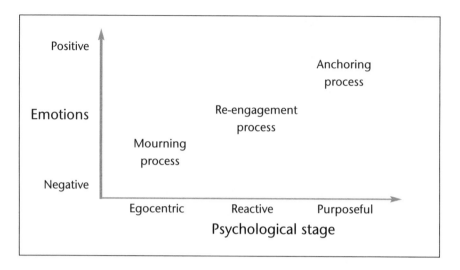

FIGURE 5.1 **Three steps of change**

- *The re-engagement process*: If the catharsis (releasing: acknowledgement and acceptance of the loss) has been well negotiated with courage and authenticity, people will want to get back into action. In this reactive/anxious phase, leaders need to avoid the "headless chicken syndrome" of uncoordinated action for its own sake.
- *The anchoring process*: In order to prevent people from falling back into the previous organizational mindset, leaders must ensure that they firmly anchor the change in the future.

We shall now go in more detail through each of those three critical phases of the leadership engagement process.

The mourning process: the "scary collective catharsis"

It is unusual for imposed change to be greeted by a wave of optimism. The band music that accompanies the news of reorganization usually sounds more like a funeral march than a Brazilian samba. The leaders and followers seem to be engaged in a negative collusion: "We can't tell them the whole story since we need to keep up morale" on the one side, and "They're not telling us something: things must be worse than expected ... prepare for the worst" on the other.

When going through shock, people need to be given the time and space to mourn. The well-known Kübler-Ross Grief Cycle, composed of five stages (denial, anger, bargaining, depression, acceptance), demonstrates this well.[2] The model was initially designed to be used with people experiencing the sudden loss of a loved one (for example parents awaiting their family at an airport who are suddenly told that the plane has crashed) and has gradually come to be used in management as well. The idea of this five-stage model is for the therapist (coach or leader) to help patients/followers move through those stages as quickly as possible. The paradox is that, if the therapist overlooks one of the stages, the patient will regularly regress to it. The same applies to leadership in imposed change conditions.

Despite knowing that people need time for grief, what do most leaders do when people engage in the mourning process (also, less poetically, called the "bitching and moaning process")?

Leaders tend to feel ill at ease in times of bitching and moaning. Usually, this is due to good intentions:

- Wanting to stay positive: "Let's not get into a negative spiral."
- Wanting to support those who are positive: "Let's not allow some moaners to sabotage everyone's morale."
- Wanting to maintain the troops' morale: "I don't have good news to bring them about this, so let's not get them started."
- Fear of the followers' reactions: "It is scary, since it might expose us [the leadership team]."
- Dealing with loyalty conflicts: "It almost feels like betraying my [leadership] team to let the followers moan about change. It is a decision we took collegially and I can't let my followers criticize it."

These are all reasonable and based on good intentions. However, blocking the mourning process will mean leaving a time bomb in the system, as well as cutting off access to people's best constructive and creative energy.

If leaders want their teams or organizations to authentically engage in change, with energy and drive rather than blind obedience, they cannot spare themselves a "group catharsis session." When leaders have the courage and determination to go through this, they usually report it as having been much easier and smoother than expected—and cathartic for them also

One of our most tense and difficult assignments was to support a newly appointed CEO in a merger forced on two institutions by a third company which had acquired them both. Everything divided those two firms: their strategies were set in opposite directions, their boards disliked each other intensely after years of personal enmities and politicking, and those were just two of many deep-rooted conflicts.

We decided, in consultation with the new CEO, to invite the top 200 leaders of the two newly merged entities for a two-day session where we could go through the mourning process with them. After the initial politically correct and well-intentioned opening address, we resolutely went for a "trousers-down" session. We decided to share all the rumors, all the negative stories heard about and amongst each other. The audience was in a state of shock: "They wouldn't dare to talk about that one ... No, please don't say this ..." One could almost read their minds in their faces. After that beginning, we asked them to "empty their bag" of sorrow and anger, and they did. Using the Zing technology tool, we ended up with more than 500 points of frustration, lots of them overlapping.[3] We called a break and clustered the grievances into ten big groups. When the participants came back, the CEO addressed each of these areas, recognizing the frustrations, sympathizing with the participants. His authenticity and integrity were such that, within a very short time, he was able to re-engage the whole audience in the next step of change: The re-engagement process.

This first step in the change engagement process is heavily influenced by negative emotions (fear for survival, territory, and habits), and has to make up for previous poor communication (rumors, absence of news, and withholding information at the top); we usually find people are in an egocentric state of mind. It is a stage close to aggressive depression, with little activity taking place, and what activity there is is usually intended to cover people's backsides, use office politics to get to the top, or more modestly just to survive. How much value is destroyed in this way every time a reorganization or merger is announced inappropriately? It is crucial to have that catharsis session so that the individual/team/organization can move towards a more positive action mode.

The first step in moving people through the mourning process is to engage them in co-creating clarity, as a way to help with the mourning process.

Co-creating clarity

When kicking-off with leadership engagement, leaders must have the courage to go after the collective catharsis. In that scary stage, it is critical for the leaders to be transparent and clear about what is up for discussion and exploration (co-creation), and what is not:

■ *What is not up for co-creation*: Often the strategy has been decided beforehand, or a decision to change (merger, organization, culture, markets, a change imposed from the outside) has been taken before the engagement process starts. If so, the whole purpose of the process should be to engage people in the change. In such cases, we recommend being clear that the strategic discussion is not up for co-creation but that time will be devoted to address doubts, questions, and concerns.
   – *Doubts*: When confronted with the brutal news of change, people may have honest doubts whether it will work or not. Such people are not necessarily intending to be difficult or negative (challenge is a sign of engagement). They just need reassurance, and will value finding that their doubts are taken seriously and with respect. There is a good chance that the few who speak up actually represent the large "silent majority."
   – *Questions*: When something new is put forward, there will be people who want to understand more. Not everything is clear to them. They will sometimes voice their questions as a push-back, as an "I don't buy-in." Don't be fooled: It is difficult to admit in front of peers "I don't get it, I don't understand it," and it sounds far better to attack and criticize. Don't fall into the trap of being defensive, just help them understand.
   – *Concerns*: Some people simply might experience fear (for survival, territory, habits) and that has to be expressed before you can reassure them.
■ *What is up for co-creation*: As a leader, when you engage your team or organization you have to be extremely clear about what you hope for, what the boundaries are. The next section gives a few examples of the different frames chosen by leaders under different circumstances. All produced solid results, and because the leaders were clear about their expectations they were able to manage the expectations of their people.

Co-creating purpose and meaning

In the fall of 2007, Nokia Devices' newly appointed SEVP for R&D, Peter Ropke, invited his new team to start with a full day's reflection on

"What should R&D's purpose and meaning be in our company?" His team worked hard all day to identify the company's hidden assumptions about R&D and to redesign their own mental models of what R&D's purpose should be. The boundaries here were quite open: Let us reinvent ourselves in line with the new organizational purpose.

In early 2008 the DSM Innovation Center brought together 50 project teams (450 people) in a circus tent. Using a tent was a signal this would be different, and it was. Hardly any PowerPoint, inspiration from the Cirque du Soleil, coffee breaks learning to juggle. These teams were the creative inspiration of the company, known as the "billion euro" community (that is the estimate of what their projects were worth). They needed to learn from each other and a two-day mass engagement was the fastest way to do it. Common tools, dream boards, idea generators, and many others—all facilitated by company executives—created inspiration, competence, and resource sharing, as well as generating a hell of a lot of energy.

Co-creating a sense of urgency

Years ago, we worked with the dean of a world-famous management school who invited the whole staff, from academics to janitors, for a solid shake-up of the institution. Suggestions ran from the "fix the coffee machines" type of recommendations to fundamental reflections on the mission, organization, and strategy of the school. People went where their energy was, to support and implement their recommendations. The purpose was also defined: "In the medium term, if we do not seriously challenge our ways of operating, we will be history. What do you recommend we should focus on?"

Validating and implementing a strategy

Between 1997 and 2002, Didier served as President of the Supervisory Board of the Tourism Office of one of Switzerland's leading resorts (that was the not-for-profit activity he had chosen to undertake). On taking office, he quickly realized that his predecessors had done tremendous work in designing strategies but, for a whole range of reasons, had been unable to fully implement them. His first move was to invite 25 business leaders from the community to help him design a new strategy. He was (and still is!) pretty ignorant of the tourism business (that is, the content) but knew that his years of consulting had provided him with a solid knowledge of process leadership (the way to create a strategy). He worked for a whole day with the 25 participants. He then invited the whole village to a two-day meeting to hear their thoughts and ask them to challenge, support, destroy misconceptions, and suggest anything they thought would help create value. The sessions attracted 150 people (the largest assembly ever gathered for such a purpose in the village) and helped validate and improve the initial plan. Following this, the participants regrouped by business (hoteliers, shop owners, ski schools, schools, farmers, etc) and reflected on how their particular interest group could concretely implement the new strategy. There were few boundaries here: the instruction was simply "please discuss, validate, amend, and implement the strategy."

Co-creating around and implementing a new strategy

The head of a private bank in Switzerland took his 150 senior managers away for two days to create a space for reflection and openness. Emotions had been running very high since an announcement that headquarters was talking about outsourcing some functions. The leaders brought out the emotions in their subgroups. By actively practicing the value-building behaviors explored in Chapter 3, they helped move people back into their control or influence zones. By the end of the first day, most people had recovered a sense of purpose and capacity to influence, and on day two the task shifted to looking for ways to implement the changes. The boundaries were clearly defined: The strategy will be implemented on a worldwide basis; let us understand why and how to implement it

Remobilizing a large community of leaders

The news had come as a bombshell: A sudden regulatory change was going to force a law firm to sever its ties to a larger network of lawyers and they would have to "go it alone" from now on. The managing partner of the network invited his 100 partners and other seniors away for two days, and courageously initiated the catharsis session. The boundary however was clear: "Let's not waste time arguing about the new regulations, which we can't do anything about. Let us redesign our future!"

The behaviors which help leaders facilitate the mourning process

People need time to understand, test, "play with the new thing" before engaging in a new direction. It is fundamental for the leaders to recognize this and display behaviors which will facilitate it. Creating the space for clarity is about:

- Listening actively: Leaders will stop selling and start listening to what their people say, at two levels:
  - *Logos* (intellectual/explicit): What is the person saying? How coherent is the argument? What do they see in what I said? What is the rationale or pseudo-rationale/logic behind what they say? Most of the real listening, however, should happen at a second level: the emotional one.
  - *Pathos* (emotional/implicit): This is usually where the gold nugget is. Unfortunately, it is often unspoken, hidden, blocked at times: it is not easy for people to lay the emotional agenda out on the table. This reluctance may be intentional (due to some hidden/political agenda), a mixture of intentional and learned response ("real men don't show emotions"), or totally unconscious (the person is not aware herself that some influence is acting in the background).
  - When brought effectively into the open, the collective "undercover" emotions of groups can be a powerful force for change. Shadow organizations of interest groups are everywhere in organizations. They are not rebel or guerilla groups; they are simply people who hope to do things better but may not have the access or permissions to act on their wishes. These shadow groups often have strong emotions about customers and purpose; they live in the shadows because there are no perceived legitimate processes or routes for them to access decision makers. Toyota encourages leaders to go directly to the line managers to communicate. Its *Yokoten* process is a viral communication system in which "everyone should know everything" and refusing to listen to others is a serious offence; it embraces contradictions presented by different groups because exploring contradiction produces the tension that will drive creativity.

An excellent example of digging into *pathos*, showing how patient and resilient a leader has to be if he is to get to the true *pathos,* is the classic movie *12 Angry Men*.[4] The film starts when 12 jurors retire to consider their verdict on a young man accused of murdering his father. The case against him seems overwhelming and on a first show of hands 11 jurors support a vote of guilty. The twelfth juror (Henry Fonda) refuses to do so, provoking the fury or incomprehension of his temporary colleagues.

"I just want to talk," he repeats on three occasions to explain why he will not condemn the young man out of hand. Then, patiently exploring the reasons that led each juror to vote "guilty," he little by little convinces them that the facts were not as clear cut as they had thought. In the end, one die-hard is left refusing to admit what has now become evident: that the inquiry has been badly led and heavily biased towards getting a conviction rather than finding who really killed the old man. In a wise blend of questioning, supporting, challenging, and summarizing, Fonda manages to break through the anger of the last juror, who bursts into tears and shares the deeply buried motive behind his determination to condemn the young man at any price. It takes the whole film to get to that point, and that is what you will sometimes face when helping people to migrate from the pseudo-rational to real *pathos*.

What role for the executives?

The active, visible, and authentic contribution of the leaders is a must in such a process. They can play different roles:

- *The leaders as facilitators*: if the number of leaders (i.e. there is a management team and not just a single boss) and followers allows, spread yourselves in groups at different tables (maximum of ten people) and engage in a purposeful dialogue on whatever theme has just been presented to the audience. Leaders will facilitate table discussions and co-create clarity and meaning at their tables, practicing the eight value-building behaviors (listen actively, ask open questions, summarize, support, challenge, clarify/contract, ask for time-out, review/feedback).
- *The leader as a conductor*: sometimes the arithmetic does not work (not enough leaders, too many people) or the management team is not yet up to this task and you would be reluctant to take a risk of exposing them. The alternative is to group the people by tables in teams and let them get on with their discussions. You need more frequent interruptions to track progress, questions, and other elements.

Other support that can be used

- *Technology*: This can be used in conjunction with either of the methods outlined above. Useful systems are provided by companies like Zing or Crystal that we mentioned earlier. They propose using laptops or keyboards that can be placed on each table. All comments from the tables are sent anonymously to a giant central screen. It is fascinating to see how much can come out of 15, 20, or 50 tables (hundreds or even thousands of comments that can then rapidly be clustered during a session break and presented back to the audience).

■ *Learning visuals*: There are a number of "business artists" who have the rare capacity to speak and understand the business jargon and logic, while depicting it in a visual form through learning posters.[5] To have a business artist sitting with the leadership team and working to understand the new direction they intend to take, what is at stake, what the strategic dilemmas are helps first of all to create clarity and alignment in the leadership team. Then, once the artist has drawn his allegory, the posters are used as material to provoke discussions. Learning visuals can also be converted into games where people chose different paths on the board. On reaching a "choice crossroads," they are asked to explore options and possibilities

Figure 5.2 shows a draft of a poster produced by Richard Erickson to help groups of participants discuss and candidly explore how they perceive their team (and in a second discussion, their company)

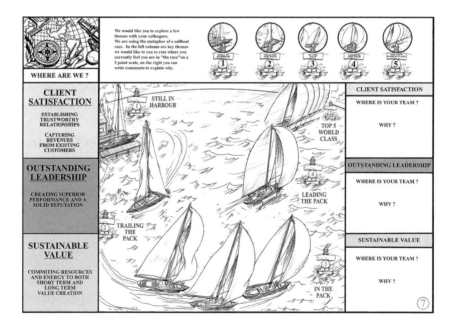

FIGURE 5.2 **Learning poster**

performance. Using an analogy (in this case a sailing competition) usually helps engage people in the discussion. Then, if well coached, participants will rapidly explore why they have different views on the subject and come to increased clarity. The best use we have seen of Richard's work is when the drawings are compiled into logbooks for participants so that they can discuss them lower down the line with their own people.

■ *Business simulations*: Business simulations, when properly designed, add significant value to the leadership engagement process. Properly designed, in our view, means not necessarily computer driven but active immersion learning that involves real consumer demands, customers (usually represented by actors), and multiple changes of landscape. They provide an opportunity to observe, reflect on, review, and enhance behavior, as well as giving participants an experience that will be used further down the engagement road as a shared, common memory of a successful moment and of pitfalls to avoid: it provides clear lessons that are engrained into the new team/organization's structure. A shared defining moment has been proved to contribute to community building.

We have over the years been third parties to a great example, as we participate in a multi-part process in which another training supplier is also engaged. This supplier uses a simulation involving a character called Moe. When the participants join us on the third module of a four-part process, the topic over dinner on the night before we start is always Moe, and the effect he, she, or it had. Each person has had to deal with Moe on Module 1 and although the results are varied, the collective memory of a highly challenging situation is a powerful stimulant to bridging and bonding.

■ *Criteria for supporting activities*: There are many activities that can be designed to support engagement. These range from simple, widely used, but still relevant team-development tasks such as distributing 30 cards with different pieces of information among team members and asking them to deduce the answer to questions like "Who owns the leopard?" or "Who grows apples?" At the other end of the scale there are multi-day computer-based strategic simulations where teams build portfolios and position themselves to gain competitive advantage in multiple markets. When designing a new simulation, or choosing which one to use from a portfolio of existing challenges, it is vital to explore the following questions:

– *Do we really need a simulation*? Is there a better way to support the desired engagement, for example by using discussions about real issues as the vehicle for learning, or by observing a team in action on a real business problem? What is the explicit learning that is required? How does it fit into the flow of a program or the wider learning process?

- *What system will be used in the simulation to measure results and provide a feedback mechanism on the actions of the group?* This could be anything from completing the task in the quickest time to scoring points or raising money to building sustainable value. However it is vital that whatever rating system is used provides a clear differentiation between those who apply the behaviors or learning principles well and those teams that are simply lucky. A mistake often made by novice designers is to think of a fun/exciting/creative activity and then build an exercise around it. Without a carefully crafted rating mechanism, such activities are little more than games. Conversely, a consistent rating mechanism allows benchmarks to be set, league tables to be created, and world records to be beaten. People need to be able to experience the connection between their behavior and value creation and destruction.

- *What is the context of the simulation?* Whilst it may seem attractive to develop a simulation for a particular business or industry (one that reproduces the type of business as closely as possible), there are disadvantages in this approach. One danger is that individuals may have particular expertise and so take a dominant role as content leaders, thus unbalancing the dynamics of the team and making success dependent less on how the team is operating than on the specialist skills of an individual. A greater threat however is the difficulty of building a simulation robust enough to withstand expert scrutiny. If a team fails, they are often tempted to look outside their own actions for the reason. Then the simulation can be an easy target, with defenses like "our business isn't exactly like that," "factor x is much more important than factor y in real life but not in this exercise," or "we wouldn't operate in those markets in reality." Taking the context of the simulation to a neutral/analogous environment limits the dangers of content expertise or "blame the game" syndrome.

- *How much time do we have?* A good rule of thumb is that for every hour of simulation activity, one hour of review or feedback time should be scheduled. On shorter simulations, this can be in one block at the end, though on longer ones it is often appropriate to have breaks in the action for reviewing. This allows a team to go through a continuous development cycle, and experience the immediate performance improvements that come from high-quality reviews. Without in-depth reviews, simulations can be fun and may help people bond, but rarely deliver lasting learning.

- *Can the simulation run itself?* When people are under pressure to perform in a simulation, their conditioned response may be to seek help from an expert or authority figure (this instinct is much stronger in some company cultures than others). The figure most immediately available is normally the coach, observer, or facilitator. If he or she gets drawn into answering queries, a pattern of dependency can rapidly form where a constant barrage of "Can we do this?" questions comes from the team. Success in the task is then a function of how well the facilitator answers the queries rather than of the combined efforts of the team. Failure can also be blamed on the coach rather than the team. If the simulation needs constant inputs from the facilitators, then facilitators will consciously or unconsciously influence the result. A better alternative is a "tight" brief where all options are covered and constraints and penalties clearly set out. A good test is whether the observer can answer any question by saying: "All the information you need is in the brief." Of course, to maintain credibility, the information does have to be in there, or be something that can be found out by experimentation, curiosity, or cooperation.

- *What level of activity do we want?* Care must be taken to build into the simulation the right level of activity to support the learning. Some exercises will deliberately create conditions where there is just too much to do. This will illustrate the importance of taking a time-out, stepping back, and identifying priorities based on clarity of purpose. Others will be designed to give a feeling that there isn't enough to keep a team fully occupied; these are a powerful way of illustrating reactive behavior. Some teams will slow down, relax, and make the activity fill the time. Others will take refuge in needless activity to reduce their anxiety at achieving less than they could; this can be the springboard for a review focusing on "assumed usefulness." In these lower-activity simulations there should be ways for people to use the space to reconnect with the purpose and ask "how can I or we add value at this moment?" and then use the opportunity presented to find how to purposefully reallocate resources.

   – *How does the simulation contribute to the overall energy of the program or process?* Do we want a big finale to give a sense of community? Would a public competition or demonstration of results be appropriate, or should the simulation be a low-key affair to support a specific learning point? An important question to answer is: "What happens if the team fails: what knock-on effect will that have?"

■ The result of a simulation will only be as good as the review. If the whole review is spent talking about details of the exercise so that people can understand what was going on, then the opportunity for learning will be lost. Some time will be needed to replay events, but this must be carefully managed. If too much time has to be spent unpacking the content instead of looking at the team's behavior and dynamics, then the exercise has been poorly designed. Occasionally, and especially on longer multi-team challenges, there may be a level of complexity that needs to be discussed; in this case a separate plenary session before the review can be very useful. This is an opportunity to "kill the game," getting all the unanswered technical questions out of the way so as to free the review period to focus on the learning. Another pitfall common to inexperienced coaches or facilitators is coming across as a "smart ass" by showing off how clever the design was. This impression may be reinforced if there is only one solution or if success would have required talents that a typical group of the participants would be unlikely to possess. Again, this is an indicator of poor design.

Conclusion

The first step of the leadership engagement process is the most critical. Participants need to feel that their leaders offer:

■ *Authenticity and transparency*: Followers will engage if they feel that their leaders put their cards on the table and give them a honest picture of where they are going and why.

■ *Courageous vulnerability*: Followers will respect and support their leaders when they see that, far from hiding on a pedestal behind a pre-choreographed show, they have come down into the arena with them, rolled up their sleeves, and entered into realistic and honest discussion with their people.

■ *Time and space to build their own sense of what is happening*: Followers are intelligent people who will value being given time and space so that they can construct their own meaning of what is happening.

- *Respect for what they feel*: The mourning process is also about leaders' showing respect for the sense of loss their people will normally have when they hear announcements about organizational changes.

THE RE-ENGAGEMENT PROCESS: "BACK TO PROBLEM-SOLVING MODE"

The re-engagement process marks the return to action. There can still be something of a "headless chicken" state (action for action's sake), but at least people are back to an operational mode. This step is more neutral ("let's get back to work") than positive and enthusiastic, and it is reactive rather than purposeful.

Continuing the delicate merger story we started earlier, it was a revelation to us all (including the CEO and all participants) to see how quickly 200 people had moved from a negative, blaming stage to an "OK, enough moaning, let's roll our sleeves up and get back to work" state of mind. We were reminded of George Bernard Shaw's famous dictum:

> People are always blaming their circumstances for what they are. I don't believe in circumstances. The people who get on in this world are the people who get up and look for the circumstances they want, and, if they can't find them, make them.[6]

People started to engage in meaningful discussions in sub-groups (each table facilitated by a member of the leadership team), getting to grips with the problems and ways to solve them. A bunch of strategy consultants who were witnessing this started to worry about the length of their contract and the billable hours their partner would be able to charge to the client! In two days, the place had gone from night to day, from negative and paralyzed to a place of action and problem solving.

The re-engagement process is about precisely that: Pull people back into action after they are through the last stage of Elisabeth Kübler-Ross's model, the acceptance phase. Professionals are unhappy when they cannot do the work they chose to do. This is even more the case with knowledge workers. Once the leaders have facilitated the catharsis and removed the roadblock of negativity, people go back to problem-solving mode with renewed determination and energy.

This process is really what allows rapid recovery for masses of people.

It may be that recovery skills are the major competitive weapon in this open space world.

Change mourners into active problem solvers

The second step of the engagement process is about re-engaging in active problem solving. We will not go on at length about techniques for problem-solving since it is a day-to-day occupation for professionals.

We will, however, mention one tool we have again and again found useful to re-engage people into action. This is the Open Space Technology, which is already used by many and is widely celebrated in the excellent *Handbook of Large Group Methods* by Barbara Bunker and Billie Alban.[7]

It is widely agreed that Harrison Owen invented the Open Space Technology around 1986. At large seminars and conventions he was repeatedly surprised to find that the time when the energy peaked was during breaks and meals. Following a similar reasoning to ours (one-way delivery meetings don't unleash creativity or energy), he thought about ways to instill "break energy" into the plenary session.

In short, an Open Space functions in the following manner:

1   Divide people among tables (groups of up to eight to ten).
2   Announce what the topic/theme of the Open Space will be. It can be wide-ranging (saving this institution) or more focused (how do we implement the new strategy). It is important however, as stressed earlier, to clearly mark the boundaries (clarity!). The themes may lead to exploration, problem solving, decision/consensus reaching.
3   Explain the process to the audience (see next steps).
4   Ask each table to come with one or two ideas (you may leave this number open but the session might lose focus) that people on the table will discuss passionately.
5   Give the tables anything from 20 to 45 minutes to agree on the key themes each has selected. Then ask the tables to appoint proponents (also called conveners) to sell each idea to the audience. One or two minutes at most is allowed per speech (called the sales pitch, which has to be short, pacy, and clear).
6   If some tables have similar topics to propose, group the themes.
7   When all themes have been proposed, the conveners invite to their tables the people in the audience who are interested in the topic.

These people (the visitors, sometimes called the bees) are free (law of two feet) to stay and discuss or move to another table. Some tables/themes will attract many people (you may want to limit the number to 15–20, then channel visitors to another table or invite people to come back later, so that the discussion is still manageable). Other tables won't have many customers; that is the "sanction of the market"—if you are a single-issue campaigner convinced that the first thing we must do to save this institution is fix the coffee machines, you may be up for a bit of loneliness. But that is fine as well. Never, ever attempt to dismiss, ridicule, or prohibit expression and subsequent discussion of an issue. If the coffee machine is all that some participants can see, that is a quick fix— "low-hanging fruit"—that can rapidly be solved.

8 If there are too many themes, you may want to run two or more rounds.

9 In the early stages, visitors go where their energy is and conveners facilitate the meeting.

10 Before the end, set plenty of time aside for the conveners to summarize the discussions held under their leadership. Typically, five types of outcomes can be expected:
   a) The discussion was a valuable exploration of a theme which will need to be developed in the future (or which led nowhere so that the participants decided to kill the idea).
   b) The discussion ended up with a concrete proposal which now needs to be taken to a higher level for decision.
   c) The discussion produced a concrete action plan which will be followed after the meeting.
   d) The discussion ended up by resolving a conflict.
   e) The discussion resulted in clarity and understanding being (co)created around a topic.

11 Several ways of sharing results are then possible:
   a) Market place: People walk around the tables, where the conveners explain the outcome of their table work.
   b) Each convener publicly summarizes the outcome.
   c) The leader or leadership team, after being briefed by the conveners, summarizes for the participants what they will take away from all the discussions.
   d) The table groups create visuals/collages that are framed and hung in a gallery, with one individual from the team by each visual to explain and explore.

The critical step here is to motivate people to get back to work and re-engage in creative and positive problem solving. This step is designed to re-empower people and give them the feeling of purpose and influence (see Chapter 4) that they might have lost with the change announcement.

THE ANCHORING PROCESS: BONDING VERSUS BRIDGING

To the best of our knowledge, the first person who coined the term "bonding versus bridging" is LBS's Professor Lynda Gratton.[8]

All leaders involved in mergers, acquisitions, and other "reorgs" know this: It is vital to project people forward into a dream which is more compelling than their past situation was comforting! Antonio Damasio calls this creating a "memory for the Future," a forward-looking identity that will propel us to where we want to be.[9]

During times of merger, people will constantly refer to each other as an "ex-this" or an "ex-that," no matter how sexy the new brand is. This is a natural human attitude. Human beings are social animals. When threatened in their survival, territory, or habits, they will look for protection in their past: past habits, past culture, past social group or tribe. Not only will they try to retain all they can of the past but they will also tend to exclude the new members who were not part of their common history.

Like the body, they will try to reject or neutralize the transplants. This is the bridging versus bonding reflex. Humans feeling threatened in their identity (territory), job, position (survival), or culture (habits) will tend to close ranks with those who think, act, and believe like them. They will even find great moral satisfaction in "killing common enemies" (or inventing them if they don't have any). This is the bonding mechanism. It looks good (people are coming together, they seem to have a good time in each others' company) but it is mainly based on the rejection of a common enemy: their new colleagues in the merged entity. Adolf Hitler and other butchers in history understood this powerful way of manipulating crowds.

The "bridging mechanism" is what leaders need to create in new situations, contexts, cultures, or organizations. Bridging is the opposite of building silos and protective walls. People engage with each other, moving away from aggressiveness or cold neutrality, they are prepared to take risks with and trust each other.

How can leaders encourage people to move from bonding towards bridging? The key to moving people from reverting to (sometimes revering) the past towards engaging in the future is to create a strong and positive "emotional anchor" about the future. Taking a simplistic example, if you are like Sylvester Stallone in *Cliffhanger* (yes, this book was in danger of becoming too boringly serious), desperately clinging to a steep wall high above the ground, the situation might feel pretty uncomfortable.[10] You might rightly believe that there is a way to get out of it, but suppose you heard some "smart ass" (sorry, adapting to our new cultural level) shouting: "Come on, throw yourself back into the void, and just spin round: there's a safe platform right behind you that you'll land on!" We bet you would freeze and demand a more solid argument before letting go of your precarious security (the old situation) and going for that "leap of faith" towards safety (a new better future). That is exactly what engaging leaders need to understand when they ask their people to stop bonding and looking at the past and instead to start bridging towards a better future. "We stood on the edge of a precipice and jumped into the void." Keeping the tension alive and visible to all may be the route to powerful creative insight

How to communicate this? The discoveries of William Schutz, an American psychologist in the 1960s, shed some light on this.[11] In his research, Will Schutz found that people have three very different sets of needs, established in childhood, which drive them to differing degrees. These are the three emotional spaces we briefly referred to in our discussion of fears:

- *Inclusion needs*: People need to feel socially significant. Ignore that and you have planted the seeds of a difficult relationship. People with high inclusion needs like to come together, to ask for and be asked for opinions, they feel important when invited to attend a meeting. When creating their bridging process, leaders must pay a great deal of attention to not leaving people out, testing the opinions of as many people as possible, ensuring that everybody feels heard and listened to. However a balance is needed; leaders who focus too much on inclusion behavior can be paralyzed by an inability to take a decision until "everybody is on board."
- *Control needs*: People need to feel in control, or at least that there is "a pilot on the plane." If you seem hesitant about what to do, show too much insecurity about your choices, they will look elsewhere for guidance. Followers with high control needs are competency driven; they will not hesitate to step boldly in and take charge, and are usually well equipped to do so. When you are launching the bridging process, they

111

will need you to be well prepared and to make out a convincing case for the new direction. The downside is of course that they find it difficult to let go of power, end up micro-managing, and alienate the goodwill of those who would also like to be influential.

■ *Affection/openness needs*: Some people need to like those who want to direct them. People with high affection needs like intimacy, closeness, authenticity, and openness. They accept the influence of warm-hearted, charismatic leaders and try to influence others in the same way. Affection-driven people will go out of their way to be personable, authentic, and caring towards others. They also have a tendency to rescue people. The reverse of the coin is that they may be conflict averse and find it difficult to be the bearer of bad news.

Engaging leaders understand that different people around them have different needs. They do not act in ways alien to their characters; they simply learn a new language and behavior, and speak or act accordingly in order to connect with their people. They match their audience as far as possible. A leader who is affection driven knows that, when he needs to move an audience towards bridging, he has to meet the inclusion needs of some of his followers, giving significance to them and inviting them in. Yet to others he needs to display respect for competence and offer structured, well-prepared, and convincing arguments (to meet control needs), while at the same time being true to his own preference, which is about being authentic and connecting. The dilemma is obvious and difficult. "Do you mean I have to act?" is a question we are frequently asked. The answer is to experiment until you feel comfortable with this "new language" or, as Alcoholics Anonymous say, "Fake it 'til you make it!"

This is a first step towards the bridging mechanism: understand the different fundamental needs that may drive your audience. Another two components are vital: Describe a future state in both an intellectually compelling and an emotionally engaging way.

Intellectually compelling

You will not get many people on board in your attempt to create a convincing future if you are not intellectually compelling. Robustness of the plan, a well-prepared message, intellectual coherence should all be part of the plan. In the multiple-Oscar-winning film *Gandhi* (we are now upgrading our reference list), Sir Ben (as the English in their own caste system still like to call their heroes) portrays a milestone in Gandhi's life: his first speech to the Indian National Congress.[12] In that scene, Gandhi is far from being the charismatic leader he became later. Set up for failure by jealous opponents, he is invited on stage to speak after the most eloquent speaker on the subcontinent. When his turn has come, the master of ceremonies introduces him in a tone which suggests "and now for those of you who wish to take a break, Mr Gandhi, an obscure lawyer from South Africa, will say a few words." As expected, people stand up and start moving towards the doors when the shy and unknown Gandhi starts to speak. The first impression—his diffident voice, unimpressive costume, and the glasses he painfully manages to fix on his nose—has everyone heading out of the chamber. But within two minutes the clarity and robustness of his message have fixed the audience on what he is saying. They stop talking, start to listen, and sit down to hear the small, apparently insignificant man talking on the podium. The speech, simply argued and intellectually robust, wipes away the dissent and confusion that have marked the session, and as he finishes they rise in a standing ovation.

Emotionally engaging

A quote from the famous French aviation pioneer, poet, and novelist, Antoine de St. Exupery[13] epitomizes the strength of emotional engagement: "If you want to build a ship, don't drum up the men to gather wood, divide the work, and give orders. Instead, teach them to yearn for the vast and endless sea." All recent research seems to agree on the point that humans make decisions on an emotional basis more than on a rational one. Emotion is what moves people, even in the most extreme situations. Take the unusual case of hostage takers and negotiators. Well-trained negotiators know that they must avoid being dragged into a pseudo-intellectual debate with such people. They would lock themselves into an endless argument. On the contrary, they must seek to develop a dialogue based on emotion. They need to build a bridge to the hostage takers' emotional agenda. If they manage to connect emotionally with their counterparts, then they have a chance to succeed. The same goes with less criminal and better-intended human beings, our colleagues. Just connecting with them intellectually is our license to operate. But the thing that will invite them to engage is the emotional connection we establish with them.

We will never forget a retreat we had planned with a Brazilian bank executive and his team at Didier's home on the seashore of Salvador de Bahia. The management team (12 people) was in trouble: there was huge pressure upon them to perform, they had been ostracized by other members of the bank, and their internal dynamics were, to say the least, not of the best. Our client was recognized as a competent professional but was unable to create an engaging and performance-driven atmosphere. Full of good intentions, he kicked off the meeting in the living room with a long, intellectual, boring speech lasting 25 minutes, when the plan had prescribed a rapid and vitalizing five-minute introduction. During the speech, we could sense the feeling of dull misery creeping over his listeners. "Here he goes again, but I am not going to say anything" was the thought one could read on their faces.

When he had finished, we needed shock therapy to move away from fake, intellectual engagement to a real, emotionally meaningful session. Didier thanked him, asked the audience if they had any comments and how they felt about the intro. As expected, the "corporately correct" jargon was dished up, with a sauce of non-committal reserve on top. When they were done, five minutes later, Didier stood up and walked towards the door: "Well thank you, everything is nice and rosy. I don't think you need us any more, if that is the level of integrity and authenticity we are going to operate at for the next three days."

The listeners started to go into shock. Didier turned to the leader and politely asked: "How long do you think you have been talking for?" "Five minutes, as planned," he said. He then got the feedback on the length and draining impact of his speech. People didn't pull their punches; they were livid. That defining moment was caught by the leader, who bravely stood up, thanked Didier for the feedback and said that this was exactly what he wanted the next days to look like. The session, which had started at 5 pm and was scheduled to end at 6, ended four hours later. The participants had been intensely involved, lowering their guard and engaging in honest and constructive feedback. The next two days were a genuine pleasure (how many of you have run efficient management meetings sitting in crystal-clear, 28° seawater in a Brazilian lagoon, with a barbecue cooking in the background and a bit of Caipirinha to help with the creativity?). In those three days, a team that had been in a defensive bonding situation ("The rest of the bank is against us") had suddenly moved towards bridging with each other and with the rest of the institution.

Building convincing business narratives (story telling)

It is also crucial to depict a future which is engaging, so that people stop looking back to the "good old days." Many techniques can be used, and we do not intend to go into the details of each one (not wishing this book to go on for another 480 pages). One technique, story telling, made popular by Steven Denning is worth spending time on.[14] We prefer the term business narratives to story telling; that may be more acceptable to the serious people amongst you.

A book we unconditionally recommend is *From Hippos to Gazelles* by Philip Goodwin and Tony Page.[15] It provides a real-life example of how stories can support major change efforts under very difficult circumstances.

Stories are more important than strategies. You may have heard the story of what happened at one of the major US car manufacturers. The board had decided that the company would become the world's first truly global car manufacturer. The sourcing and manufacturing processes would obviously be important building blocks in that strategy. The whole top management had also intellectually committed to the plan. Years later they were all pretty upset to realize that their vision was still just a vision and not being implemented. In a moment of wisdom, instead of calling the usual consultants, the CEO invited a team of psychologists, sociologists, and anthropologists to help them understand why moving from intention to action was so difficult.

Their report was mind boggling: "The heroes," they said, "and the stories about them are all about how one site managed to outwit the other, how pretending to cooperate while sabotaging the others worked out well." It was the stories and their heroes that were real to the people; the strategy was just an illusion.

Similarly, a European bank had decided to refocus the business on the "middle market." There was only slow progress on implementing that plan however. People didn't understand why they had to abandon the things that made them proud (big, highly publicized deals where all the internal heroes were the deal makers, some of them on the board) to focus on targets that had no such glamorous ambition. The meetings at which the execs tried to sell the new strategic intent were uninspiring purgatories that seemed to lead nowhere for them or their audiences. Until the day that one of the execs came up with the following story:

Think of us as a large car manufacturer. We still need to have a

NASCAR or Formula 1 Racing Team. We learn a lot from them and they are our flagship. But manufacturers don't make any money from their racing teams. The money comes when the technology and reputation earned by the racers are translated into products for the mass market.

The penny dropped and the strategy started to make a lot of sense to the audience.

Credible leaders excel at the art of story telling. Gone are the days when we told our children the story of Snow-White and the Seven Dwarfs. Today, when asked for the hundredth version of the story, we ask them to wait a while, go to our home office, get out the overhead projector and laptop, and start projecting our Snow-White Power-Point slides 1–36! Anyone who has children, nephews, nieces, anyone who has basically had experience with a child, is familiar with the art of story telling.

A solid business story (or narrative) follows the logic of the three agendas:

■ It has a solid and simple intellectual message (a punch line). Ask anyone around the world what was the key message of Martin Luther King's famous "I have a dream" speech, and even among those who haven't seen/heard it the message has been received 5/5: "It's about the end of segregation, about equality, about respect." A solid story has therefore a clear, simple, and punchy message.
■ It is delivered with a coherent behavioral style: People don't listen to what you say (remember the old study[16] showing that only 7 percent of people's attention during a speech is given to the content while the rest goes to behaviors and emotions?), they listen to what you do. The good old "It's not *what* you said, it's *the way* that you said it" applies here as well.
■ It has a strong "emotional anchor". The following two examples will hopefully clarify the concept.

The EPFZ has done research into why some people manage to free themselves from an addiction (alcohol, tobacco, drugs, or medication) while others fail, no matter how hard they try. To simplify the results of a complex study, we can say that the ones who succeeded had first anchored their intention to quit in their emotional memory, before turning to the

FIGURE 5.3 **Addiction**

volitional memory where that intention is located (see Figure 5.3). Those who failed had tried to "take a shortcut" by anchoring their desire to quit directly into the volitional memory.

This example suggests one way to think about the emotional agenda. Another way is to share the true story of Didier's friend Angela. Her name seemed right for her: she looked like an angel when he first met her 25 years ago in South America. Like Sleeping Beauty, it seemed that all the fairies had blessed her at birth with beauty, intelligence, charm, and wealth. Life went on, and he suddenly got a call in Switzerland from Angela, whom he hadn't heard from in 20 years. She was passing through and wondered if they could catch up after so long. Didier and his wife invited her for dinner and they both remember their panic at the thought that, since Angela had had all she could want in life when she was younger, they wouldn't be able to find a good enough bottle of wine to celebrate their reunion. Their fears were realized during the meal: Angela hardly touched her glass of Bordeaux. Feeling that they had failed to please (and that was one of their best bottles), he asked her: "You don't like the wine? Shall we try a different bottle?" She looked at him in surprise:

> You haven't heard what happened to me? After I got married, I drifted into drug addiction and alcoholism. I would take cocaine as soon as I woke up, and gradually turn to alcohol towards the end of the day so that I could get to sleep. This went on for years until—I remember it as if it were yesterday—Andres, my son, came to see me on my birthday. He was eight at the time. Making a big fuss of it, he was proudly hiding something behind his back. "Mum," he said, 'I am so proud of myself, I've found just the present for you, the thing you like most on Earth, this is so much you ... I've emptied my piggy-bank but I am so happy!" The next second, he plonked a bottle of whisky on the table and ... I burst into tears. A few days later I was admitted into a rehab center, and in all my long stay there nothing hurt me as much as when Andres gave me that wake-up call.

Which story will stick more with you? The EPFZ's one or Angela's? The best way to real understanding is probably a synthesis of the two: a clear message (research shows that people who emotionally anchor their desire to give up an addiction are more likely to succeed than those who only anchor it in determination) and the emotional anchor provided by Angela's story.

Leaders who excel at story telling create an intellectually compelling and emotionally engaging picture of the future. They display coherence between *logos*, *ethos*, and *pathos*.

Every one of us probably still remembers Martin Luther King's legendary "I have a dream" speech. If you would like to show it to your children, go on www.youtube.com where several versions of it are posted.

Less famous but far more dramatic, and a perfect though tragic example of story telling by the same Reverend King, can be seen on the same website under the title: "Martin Luther King Jr's last speech." That short (one minute 16 seconds) clip is simply breathtaking in the perfection of its story-telling skills and, sadly and frighteningly, in the accuracy of its prediction. It shows Dr King in what was apparently his last public speech before his assassination. He addressed his audience brilliantly, using the three agendas:

- One very clear message (intellectual agenda/*logos*): "The goal is in sight so let us not be stopped by difficulties!"
- A perfectly matching style (behavioral agenda/*ethos*): Dr King speaks with passion. His voice, his posture, his facial expression, all work together to support his key message.
- An amazing use of symbols in order to create the persisting, unforgettable "emotional anchor" (*pathos*): "I have seen the Promised Land!" The parallel with the story of Moses (who had himself been allowed to see the land of his dream from the top of Mount Nebo before dying) is evident: Dr King is aware of the threats to his life but declares he is ready to die, since his eyes have now seen the Promised Land.

If one can forget what happened to Dr King a few hours after that speech, this clip shows a perfect example of powerful story telling.

CONCLUSION

The leadership engagement process is far more than getting the leadership team together for a few days in a fancy place. It is about:

1 Preparing the leaders to play an active and courageous role in any potential mourning process and support people throughout it.
2 Ensuring the renewed energy, produced by a healthy catharsis during the mourning process, is properly channeled towards creative problem solving.

3 Then, the capacity of leaders to draw an intellectually compelling and emotionally engaging image of the future is key in ensuring that people in the re-formed organizations build bridges towards each other instead of bonding defensively with their old relationships, still yearning for the past.

CHAPTER 6

CONCLUSION: FROM MYTHICAL HEROES TO BUSINESS LEADERS (JOSEPH CAMPBELL'S LEGACY TO BUSINESS LEADERS)

THE STORY OF MANOJ NARENDER MADNANI AND SVEN LARSEN

Manoj Narender Madnani is today a self-confident and highly successful businessman, as well as a happy husband and proud father. Narender, as his friends call him, has followed a rapid upward trajectory in finance. At the age of 38, he is the managing director of one of Europe's sharpest private investment companies.

Didier first met him 25 years ago, when he was teaching skiing during a two-year sabbatical and Narender was studying in one of Switzerland's leading international schools. Narender was a tiny, bespectacled Indian boy, sadly handicapped by a severe stutter which had become part of his identity. Of course other boys laughed at his difficulty, even voting for him to take on the chore of doing the wake-up calls in the morning, claiming that his stutter gave them an extra five minutes in bed by the time he had managed to call out their names properly.

After that, Didier did not come across Narender for years, and when he did, he felt confusedly that something had changed in the younger man. For one thing, the stutter had totally disappeared. Let us go back to where the journey of Sven and Narender began.

Sven Larsen was an unusual and original professor of English, one really passionate about his mission as an educator. One evening after dinner, he called for Narender, who at first was reluctant to go ("Bad news, what have I done wrong now? Better pretend I haven't heard him."). Indeed, that call was summoning Narender on an adventure and, as we will see, he was wise to hesitate.

But Sven is a determined man. He called louder and, once cornered, Narender had no choice but to surrender. He sat down with Sven. Being a rather direct person, the teacher challenged him: "Are you happy with your stutter? Don't you want to do anything about it?" he asked. Narender replied in a non-committal manner that it wasn't pleasant, other kids were laughing at it, but he had got used to it. Narender was once more trying to ignore the call to adventure.

Sven challenged and encouraged him further: "There is a way to get rid of it, Narender, but it will take courage and determination." Luckily these were virtues the young boy didn't lack. "I want you to volunteer for and win the next reading competition!" Narender concluded that Mr Larsen was just another person making fun of his handicap. "Is there a text you would be keen to read?" "None in particular, sir" "Well here is one for you," said Sven, handing over a text by a man called Patrick

123

Campbell and going on to describe the painful road to success of a man badly handicapped in life by his stutter.

Narender saw the benevolent and encouraging light in his professor's eyes and decided to "cross the threshold." He read, re-read, read again in a loud voice. He failed, tried again, failed again, started over again. This went on for two full weeks. By the end, he knew the whole text by heart and did not need to read it. Narender was already demonstrating one of the key traits in leadership: Recovery. He simply would not give up.

Came the day of the competition. Narender was face to face with his nightmare: his phobia about talking in public. He confesses today that he was tempted to give in and wave the white flag. This is the "moment of truth" in the hero's journey, when he meets his Nemesis.

However, while waiting to go on stage, Narender thought of the sacrifice his parents were making in sending him to Switzerland, and thought too that he did not want to disappoint Mr Larsen. So when his turn came, he confronted his fear and "went for it." A few minutes later (which of course felt like an hour to him) Narender was aware of a huge clamor coming from his fellow pupils. Not understanding why nor how, he suddenly found he was being carried in triumph on their shoulders. In one single moment he had both become a hero and won the competition.

Later on, Narender became president of his school's debating society and is one of the most self-assured individuals Didier knows.

The story of the Narenders of this world reflects almost step by step the deep, lifelong research of Joseph Campbell, who came up with the notion of the hero's journey and the "monomyth," and has since inspired both leaders and Hollywood script writers.

JOSEPH CAMPBELL

Joseph Campbell was an American anthropologist and professor of mythology.[1] Very early in his career, he developed an interest in myths, stories, and legends, and had a strong intuition that there were a lot of common features in the ways different nations, faiths, and cultures described the journey of their heroes through their paths of initiation.

In 1949 Campbell published a book, *The Hero with a Thousand Faces*, which suggested that there was indeed a founding myth common to all, which he labeled the monomyth.[2] For Campbell, myths were important since they could provide a "psychological roadmap" to guide people towards self-discovery. One passage in the book summarizes the importance of heroes and what their journey is about:

A hero ventures forth from the world of common day into a region of supernatural wonder: fabulous forces are there encountered and a decisive victory is won: the hero comes back from this mysterious adventure with the power to bestow boons on his fellow man.

Campbell's work inspired a young Hollywood script writer, Christopher Vogler, who, in the early 1990s wrote the famous seven-page "Vogler's Memo," which in turn strongly influenced the US movie industry to produce films that would appeal to the deeper nature of mankind.

Closer to the business world, a group of talented artists started to develop Campbell and Vogler's work and help managers understand that their journey through professional life is also comparable to heroic myth. David Pearl and his team, using video clips and excellent story telling, invite large groups of executives to reflect on "the leader's journey."[3]

HOW THE HERO'S JOURNEY HELPS BUSINESS LEADERS

Why do you need to know this? Anyone who has facilitated large change knows what an intellectual, physical, and emotional roller-coaster this process can be (see our comments on "the house of change"). Being an engaging leader is no exception to the rule. The hero's journey provides a remarkable description of the virtues and skills needed by today's "heroic" business leaders. It brings together, in an amazing allegory, the *logos*, *ethos*, and *pathos*, leadership's three agendas.

Recovery and deep intent

The key message of the hero's journey is not about any single step (among the 17 Campbell had described) but rather a constant "presence" throughout the adventure: recovery and deep intent.

Cast Away[4] with Tom Hanks is a great illustration of what we mean here. The survivor of an air crash is stranded on a desert island. A large part of the movie recounts his efforts to get back to society and depicts at length his capacity to recover after each failed attempt. This is based on a strong driver (deep intent): his commitment to his girlfriend, symbolized by the pocket watch she gave him just before his FedEx plane took off. We also see how bumpy the road to heroism is: When he finally manages to escape, Chuck (Tom Hanks) realizes that the whole world has given him up for dead. His beloved has married someone else with whom she has a child. Chuck once again has to demonstrate recovery capacity and rebuild a new, strong deep intent.

The capacity to recover, and the very strong driver it is based on, are the fundamentals for the hero's journey. The same applies to engaging leaders.

As a farewell, let us walk together through the main steps of Campbell's heroic journey and see if they trigger some memories for you.

The mental and emotional preparedness

This is you in the business-as-usual context.

In his seminars, Esa Saarinen[5] (the famous and unique Finnish business-philosopher) brilliantly focuses participants' minds by taking the example of Timothy McCarthy, a father of three assigned as a secret service agent to protect President Reagan in 1981. When John Hinckley Jr, who was obsessed with Jodie Foster, tried to shoot the President in Washington on 30 March, McCarthy threw himself in the line of fire without hesitating for a second (and was seriously wounded). Esa explores with his audience what internal drive may impel an ordinary man doing his daily job to suddenly act heroically. Professional and personal lives are made up of daily routines. How we live them, and how we stay mentally alert, will determine the rest of the journey. The way to engaging leadership is to listen to the inner voice which tells you that PowerPointing down at the lower echelons won't make things happen. As with Jose Luis Martinez, when he was heading Nokia Spain, there is that "leadership integrity voice" that comes and disturbs you, suggesting that there is something more courageous, determined, and heroic you could do about bringing change inside your organization. This "pre-journey" stage leads on to the next stage in Campbell's description. In the movie industry, it is the beginning of most films: a peaceful village, an ordinary day, sometimes almost a sense of boredom. When running seminars, we take the allegory of this journey and ask our audience:

- What is your business routine?
- What could the "call to adventure" be that you are about to hear?
- Describe previous calls to adventure you have received.

The call to adventure

Staying with our highly academic approach, in *Cellular* Kim Basinger is kidnapped by gangsters.[6] At one point, she manages to find an old landline, calls up a guy on his mobile phone (a random connection over which she has no choice), and desperately pleads for help. What do you think happens? The young man rejects this "call to adventure" several times before finally screwing up his courage and confronting the kidnappers. Our capacity as leaders to hear the early calls for adventure depends on our curiosity, our willingness to explore and challenge ourselves, and our deeply held beliefs and mental models. Once the call is clearly heard, do we answer it or reject it? In your journey of leadership engagement, will you have the curiosity to hear the call or will you ignore it? Wise heroes don't immediately jump with joy and rush to meet any challenge that comes along. In his remarkable movie *Million Dollar Baby*, Clint Eastwood four times refuses the invitation to coach Maggie (Hilary Swank).[7] Some of the questions we go on to ask are:

- What were your reasons for refusing past calls to adventure?
- When was that the right or wrong decision, and why?
- What did you learn and what happened next?

The defining moment (Crossing the first threshold)

This is the unique moment (the tipping point) where the leader takes a stand and makes things happen. *Walk the Line* is an excellent movie that traces the life of singer Johnny Cash. The defining moment of his career comes when, rejected by the manager he hoped would hire him and his two partners, Cash asks for just a few more minutes, throws off his Gospel music style, and takes the risk of singing something new, bold and politically incorrect.[8] He and his companions are immediately hired. We ask people:

- What made you decide to cross the threshold?
- How did it go?
- When was the result positive and when negative, and why?

The moments of doubt (Roads of trial)

After a moment of unfounded optimism (which might wrongly lead the hero to suppose that the toughest part of the journey was taking the strategic decision), disillusion will set in, problems and challenges will arise. The hero will ask herself "Why did I take this on?" and will almost wish she had not made her stand. Some questions may be asked about this:

- Describe your doubts.
- How did it feel when you shifted from "unfounded optimism" to "informed pessimism"?
- What have you learned from that process?

Facing the Nemesis/shadow (Roads of trial)

Campbell had been very much influenced by Freud and Jung. Nemesis is equivalent to Jung's shadow. A simpler description in today's language would be "our nightmare." Go back to all heroic stories; there is a crucial moment where the challenge holds up a mirror to the hero. For us, true leaders have the courage and integrity to know themselves, their noble side but also their shadow side. Nemesis lies within ourselves. In a brilliant documentary on Muhammad Ali,[9] Leon Gast shows us the iconic boxer in his 1974 fight against George Foreman. From the start, Ali dives into his deep "bag of tricks" (provoking, dancing, right-hand leads) in the hope of knocking the impressive Foreman down as quickly as possible. But none of them work. At the end of round one, Foreman is alive, kicking, and enraged. Norman Mailer, commenting on the documentary, admits: "That's the only time I ever saw fear in Ali's eyes." At the age of 32, Muhammad Ali was meeting his Nemesis, in the ring in front of a huge audience. He had the choice between defeat or dealing with his Nemesis. When attempting to bring this scenario into the business context we ask:

- What have been the Nemeses you've encountered in professional life so far?
- Why did they scare you?
- How did your Nemeses help you grow?

Nemisis, no matter how formidable it may appear, has a truly positive side: it is there so that we can grow and learn from our victory over it. This leads to the next theme: Recovery

The Recovery (Roads of trial)

As the saying goes, "Shit will happen" on our challenging journey. The key message of the hero's journey is about recovery. There would be no hero without the capacity to dream, fall, and stand up again. In *Batman Begins*, young Bruce Wayne falls into a pit.[10] His father comments: "Why do we fall? So that we can learn to pick ourselves up." Years later, his butler reminds Bruce of his father's words when the family estate burns to the ground. After the first round of Ali's fight against Foreman, Mailer tells how during the break he saw Ali talking to himself and focusing. He was determined to fight back and recover. The 32-year-old boxer decided to further provoke his younger opponent and force him to punch himself into exhaustion. In round eight, when Foreman could hardly keep on his feet from fatigue, Ali floored him with two sudden punches to regain his title. The same goes for us in business. Our capacity to recover is critical in a competitive, emerging business context where "fail faster" will become the mantra. When encouraging participants to understand this mechanism we ask:

- When defeated in the past, where did you find the strength to come back?
- How did it feel? What did you learn?

The refusal to follow (refusal to return)

This is the central theme of our book. Once she has seen the light, how can a leader then engage her troops? The hero has been successful in her journey, and at its end has hesitated to come back to the old familiar world. Finally she does so, and is now faced again with the mediocrity of those who don't know. Does this sound familiar? We have attempted to describe best practice and poor practices around that theme in this book. Just for fun, take a look at the wonderful British actor John Cleese in *Fierce Creatures*.[11] He plays an executive parachuted into a zoo, bought by accident in a mega-acquisition. The clip where he first meets his troops and tries to align them on his vision is hilarious.

The master of two worlds

This is the end of the journey; it is now time to prepare for the next. Having acquired wisdom from "the spiritual world," the hero will be readier to take on the next challenge. This is called the "driver," "life project" "*la force motrice*" or "deep intent."

In December 1998, Didier was confronted with this notion for the first time. A great fan of the Brazilian football team (his wife and children are Brazilian), he had written a note to the new coach, Wanderlei Luxemburgo, seeking to share his views on why Brazil had so badly underperformed on 12 July in the final against France. The Brazilian coach invited him to meet someone who was a living legend in Brazil, Suzy Fleury, the psychologist who worked with the squad. When he arrived at her home at 9.00 sharp as planned, Suzy greeted him and said: "I have booked the whole day for this meeting. But before proceeding, I would like to understand how this will contribute to your life project."

Didier was in a state of shock. "My what?" "Don't you have a life project? Something for which you live passionately? That gets you out of bed every morning with energy? The garden is large, go and have a walk. Come back when you've found it." Didier felt like asking if she had a tent to camp in and food for a few weeks. He went for the walk and came back with a sense of new-found peace: "Yes, I do know what feeds my energy and passion in life: my wonderful wife and our three children." Suzy smiled and they had a fruitful meeting.

The deep intent is poignantly visible in *Million Dollar Baby*: Clint Eastwood (Frankie Dunn) is destroyed by guilt. He had agreed to send Maggie to a fight (the final of the world championship) which he knew she wasn't ready for. She is now paralyzed and has asked him to help her end her life. Morgan Freeman (Scrap) talks about deep intent: "People die everyday, mopping floors, washing dishes and you know what their last thought is? I never got my shot ... If she dies today, her last thought will be: 'I think I did all right.'" Very moving. It is fundamental to each human being—and even more to those in a position to lead others—to understand what drives them. That intent may change dramatically (remember in the movie *Gladiator*, Maximus's initial intent after winning the war is to return to his wife and child.[12] After both are executed, his deep intent changes dramatically), and we may have several (a professional intent and a private-life one). Nevertheless it is critical, especially in a leadership position, to understand what drives us and others. The driver/deep intent/life project is what feeds the hero's energy along the journey. It is the source of his recovery capacity.

Resolutely determined in leading your organization during the rough times of change, you will be on your heroic journey. During our seminars, Olivier Lacheze Beer (of David Pearl Group) looks at the audience with respect and reminds them: "You are the main actors of your lives' movies. You are the heroes. This is your leadership journey!" Have a safe journey and enjoy the ride! Thank you for having read this to its end.

NOTES, REFERENCES, BIBLIOGRAPHY AND FILMOGRAPHY

HOW THIS BOOK WAS CONCEIVED

1. IMD, the International Institute for Management Development based in Lausanne (Switzerland—www.imd.ch) is one of the world's leading business schools. It ranked second on the *Financial Times* Survey for Executive Customer Education in 2007 .

2. Villars sur Ollon is one of Switzerland's most inspiring ski resorts, in Chris and Didier's biased opinions, since they both chose to live there (see www.villars.ch). During Didier's tenure as President of the Tourist Office (a part-time, not-for-profit activity) it went from near bankruptcy to one of Switzerland's top ten ski destinations (*Bilan*, October 1999).

   Mobilizing Teams International (www.mobilizingteams.com): MTI is a network of independent business consultants specializing in leadership development, leading change, strategy implementation, organization development, and team building. MTI facilitates change of behavior in individuals and teams, helping people to adjust their behavior to new contexts as well as building and releasing energy throughout organizations. MTI's competitive edge comes from its ability to orchestrate the triad of strategic, behavioral, and emotional agendas: *logos, ethos,* and *pathos*. MTI creates the conditions to effectively confront business and personal dilemmas and produce sustainable behavioral change.

3. R. Pascale, M. Millemann, and L. Gioja (2001) *Surfing the Edge of Chaos* (Texere Publishing) is a thought-provoking book that attempts to reconcile some of the well-known chaos theories with business logic.

PURPOSE AND STRUCTURE

1. T. Osono, H. Takeuchi, and N. Shimizu (June 2008) "The contradictions that drive Toyota's success," *Harvard Business Review*, June (Reprint R0806F).

1. THE NEED FOR A NEW LEADERSHIP STYLE

1. J. C. Rufin's (2001) *L'Empire et les nouveaux Barbares*, 3rd edn (Lattes) is a visionary book, drawing a parallel between the isolationist reflex of the Roman Empire, which caused it to lose sight and understanding of its enemies (the Barbarians) and ultimately led to its destruction, and the Occidental democracies which, Rufin suggests, are building a modern version of Hadrian's Wall today.

   A. Toffler (1984) *The Third Wave* (Bantam). Alvin Toffler is a writer and "futurist." His opinions and visions of the future became very well known and influential in the 1980s and 1990s. The "third wave" in the title of one of his most famous book refers to the "post-industrial society" which, he claims, will be the society of the "information age."

   P. Senge (1994) *The Fifth Discipline: The art and practice of the learning organization* (Currency). Senge's book is a must-have in the library of any leader. It is still very relevant nowadays. The five disciplines advocated by Senge are: 1) Building shared vision, 2) Understanding and using mental models, 3) Team learning, 4) Personal mastery, and 5) Systems thinking.

   J. Jaworski (1996) *Synchronicity: The inner path of leadership* (Berret-Koehler). Joe Jaworski, starting with the amazing example of his father, the prosecutor in charge of investigating Nixon's Watergate, proposes an inspiring version of leadership that is close to servant leadership.

2. T. L. Friedman (2006) *The World is Flat: A brief history of the 21st century* (Farrar, Straus and Giroux). A visionary book in which Friedman, a regular contributor to the *Herald Tribune*, explores the impact of globalization.

3. Frederick Winslow Taylor (1856–1915) was one of the leaders of the "efficiency movement." Believing that workers had only a limited ability to understand their roles, Taylor advocated splitting their tasks in the simplest, most repetitive way possible, in order to avoid mistakes and speed up the learning curve. This is turn led to important layers of hierarchies, of people who were there to coordinate the simpler workers doing simple tasks, and people to coordinate and supervise those who were coordinating... and so on ...

4. J. A. Belasco and R. C. Stayer (1994) *Flight of the Buffalo: Soaring to excellence, learning to let employees lead*, new edn (Grand Central Publishing). Using the metaphor of buffalos and wild geese, Belasco and Stayer explain that buffalos became an endangered species because of their collusion in a highly hierarchical type of leadership/followership. They contrast this style to wild geese, much more organic and less authoritarian.

   R. C. Stayer (1990) "How I learned to let my workers lead," *Harvard Business Review*, November/December (Reprint 90610) is a great summary of *Flight of the Buffalo*. Advocates of the "get to the point fast" style of reading would do well to buy that first.

5. This was a term used in a conversation with one of the authors by the then IMD Director of MBA courses Kamran Kashani, when he was attempting to radically transform the Institute's MBA approach.

6. With Didier's eternal gratitude to the late IMD Professor Werner Kettelhöhn who, in the name of Latin solidarity (Didier's grandmother is originally from Colombia, yes, like Shakira!) spent hours and hours of out-of-class time in

Lausanne's "White Horse Pub" preparing him successfully to pass IMD's useless Basic Test on this useless subject.

7. A. Fabarez (1996) "Vendredi chaotique: Wall Street perd 3%," *L'AGEFI*.

8. Don Taps and Anthony D. Williams (2008) *Wikinomics: How mass collaboration changes everything*, expanded edn (Portfolio) is a visionary book on how the new communication technologies reshape the competitive business and social landscape. A must-read!

9. Barbara L. Fredrickson and Marcial F. Losada (2005) "Positive affect and the complex dynamics of human flourishing," *American Psychologist*, Vol. 60, No. 7, October, pp. 678–86.

10. INSEAD (www.insead.edu) is one of Europe's leading business schools and is located in Fontainebleau (France) while also having a campus in Singapore. Solvay Business School (www.solvay.edu) in Brussels is Belgium's leading business school. ELP (Executive Learning Partnership) is one of our closest partners in business. Its members, who describe themselves as "strategy and learning architects" (www.elpnetwork.com), excel in the art of designing innovative leadership development programs, specially aiming at the intellectual/strategic agenda.

11. Robert Fritz (2006) *The Path of Least Resistance: Learning to become the creative force in your own life* (Free Press).

12. O. Harari (2006) *Break From the Pack: How to compete in a copycat economy* (FT Press). In this excellent and refreshing book, Harari proposes recipes to get out of the commodization Hell which he labels the "copycat economy." His recipe is to encourage employees to remain "curious, cool and crazy," a culture which he calls "disciplined lunacy."

13. Claes F. Janssen (1996) *The Four Rooms of Change* (Wahlström & Widstrand). Unfortunately, most of Janssen's books are only available in Swedish. We advise readers to take a look at his website where his thoughts are well developed (www.claesjanssen.com).

    William Bridges (2004) *Transitions: Making sense of life's changes*, revised 25th anniversary edition (Da Capo Press). This is a deep and very revealing book on how people successfully migrate through challenging moments of their lives.

14. http://en.wikipedia.org/wiki/Modes_of_persuasion (accessed 29 September 2007).

15. S. Covey and R. Merrill (2006) *The Speed of Trust: The one thing that changes everything* (Free Press). In this excellent book, Covey and Merrill emphasize trust as a key competitive advantage in tomorrow's knowledge-driven competition. A lack of trust dramatically slows down communication and information sharing.

16. Gottman, J. (2007) "Making relationships work," *Harvard Business Review*, December (Reprint R0712B)

2. CO-CREATING CLARITY AND PURPOSE AROUND THE INTELLECTUAL AGENDA

1. Stefan Stern (2006) "My two weeks in hell with the tortured soul of Dell," *Financial Times*, 7 November.

2. J. Collins and J. Porras (1994) *Built to Last: Successful habits of visionary companies* (HarperBusiness). Collins and Porras seem to have learned from the painful experience of Waterman and Peters, whose 1982 book *In Search of Excellence* had acclaimed 43 companies as excellent, of which a third were in severe difficulties or had disappeared five years after the publication of their study (see *BusinessWeek*, 5 November 1984, "Oops, who's excellent now?"). They first carefully researched business history to see which companies could claim the title of excellent (called visionaries in their book). The companies had to have been successful since at least 1950 (the average founding date of the firms they selected was 1897). Collins and Porras claimed their study destroyed 12 "myths" about successful companies:

    1) "It takes a great idea to start a great company." WRONG: In fact the organizations they studied "started slowly and won the long race."
    2) "Great charismatic leaders are needed," WRONG: "Clock builders are more powerful than time tellers," as Collins and Porras put it in *Built to Last*. Collins later developed this idea in another solid piece of work, *From Good to Great* (HarperCollins, 2001). In this book, he demonstrates that leaders who are successful in the long term are animated by "humility and fierce resolve" rather than by ego and a desire to shine.
    3) "Maximizing profits is the essence." WRONG again: Sustainably successful firms are driven by "core values and sense of purpose."
    4) "There is a correct set of core values," WRONG: What matters is living those values rather than looking for a perfect set of them.
    5) "The only constant is change." NOT EXACTLY, Collins and Porras reply. Maintaining the core values *whilst constantly seeking to improve* is the right balance.
    6) "Play it safe" should be the rule. WRONG: BHAGs are needed (Big Hairy Audacious Goals).
    7) Such companies "must be a great place to work for everyone." WRONG: Great firms have a solid set of values. When recruiting staff they state these values openly and make it clear that not everyone should/will like them.
    8) There is a "need for brilliant and complex strategies." WRONG: "Trial and error, experimentation and learning from mistakes" are the basis of successful companies.
    9) Successful companies "hire outside CEOs to stimulate change." WRONG: Collins and Porras conclude that "insiders know better."
    10) "Focus primarily on beating competition." DANGEROUS MISTAKE, they claim. As in sports, "a focus on beating yourself" is the foundation for long-term success.
    11) Decisiveness implies an "either–or state of mind," WRONG: "Both–and" is more efficient.
    12) "Companies need a visionary statement to become visionaries." WRONG: as Stefan Stern also suggests in his article, "exemplifying the value statement" is much more important.

    See: Tom Peters and Robert Waterman (1982) *In Search of Excellence: Lessons from America's Best Run Companies* (Warner Books); J. Collins (2001) *Good to Great* (HarperCollins).

3. Francisco Varela (1946–2001) was a Chilean biologist, neurologist, and philosopher. Prior to his premature death, he was leading a research group at the prestigious French CNRS.

    His comments on information are quoted by Margaret J. Wheatley and Myron Kellner-Rogers in "Self-organization: the irresistible future of organizing" (*Strategy and Leadership*, fall 1996)

4. Quoted by Margaret J. Wheatley and Myron Kellner-Rogers, "Can one lead change? Bringing life to organizational change," (1996), from Margaret Wheatley's website at http://www.berkana.org/, quoted with her permission.

5. E. Osono, N. Shimizu, and H. Takeuchi (2008) *Extreme Toyota: Radical contradictions that drive success at the world's best manufacturer* (Wiley) is the book on which the article on "The contradictions that drive Toyota's success," (cited earlier) was based.

6. Carl Jung (1875–1961) was a Swiss psychiatrist who was an early follower of Sigmund Freud, until they fell out over a theoretical disagreement. Amongst Jung's many writings and discoveries, his work on archetypes remains famous. Building upon his 1921 book *Psychological Types*, Katharine Cook Briggs and her daughter Isabel Briggs Myers developed a questionnaire which would help to rapidly define a person's main archetype. The MBTI (Myers-Briggs Type Indicator), which they first proposed during the Second World War, has become one of the world's most widely used psychometric instruments.

    Also see David Keirsey (ttp://keirsey.com) for a more complete explanation of these temperaments. Keirsey proposes a very useful clustering in four main "families" of the 16 MBTI types. The SJ (the sensing/judging preference, also called the guardians, or traditionalists, loyalists) value loyalty, honesty, and order. They bring calm, balance, and serenity. They need, facts, figures, data, clarity on roles, rules, and procedures to be at their best. At the extreme, their need for certainty may provoke paralysis by analysis in their team.

    The SP (the sensing/perceiving preference, also called the artisans, troubleshooters or negotiators) value freedom to experiment, flexibility, action and finding solutions. They bring energy, options, and practicality. They need freedom to try, engage in trial and error, action and success to be at their best. At the extreme, their need for action may transform them into "headless chickens" or troublemakers (instead of troubleshooters), and they have a tendency to "shoot from the hip."

    The NT (iNtuitive/thinking preference, also called the rationals, architects or visionaries) value integrity, coherence, and logic. They bring objectivity and clarity about the purpose and vision. They need clarity about the aim, the big picture, and have to understand the compelling reasons for actions in order to be at their best. At the extreme, their need for objective and detached logic may mislead others into seeing them as cold and detached from reality, lacking empathy, or too theoretical.

    Finally, the NF (iNtuitive/feeling preference, also called the idealists, catalysts or healers) bring authenticity, compassion, and harmony. They work through understanding, coordination, and facilitation. They need harmony, good relations, and the "feelgood" ambiance in order to be at their best. At the extreme, their need for harmony may cause them to block "positive abrasion," focus on relationship at the expense of result, or to be ill at ease with conflict.

7. J. Gray (2004) *Consciousness: Creeping up on the hard problem* (Oxford University Press).

8. Earnings before interest, taxes, depreciation and amortization (EBITDA) is a widely used metric of a company's profitability.

9. John McWhirter is the managing partner of sensory systems (http://www.sensorysystems.co.uk).

10. R. F. Baumeister, E. Bratslavsky, C. Finkenauer, and K. Vohs (2001) "Bad is stronger than good," *Review of General Psychology*, Vol. 5, No. 4, December, pp. 323–70

11. Surowiecki, J. (2005) *The Wisdom of Crowds* (Anchor).

12. Surowiecki's book begins with the story of the British scientist Francis Galton, who believed that decisions taken by a crowd would never be as good as those of experts, and therefore that democracy would never be as efficient as a government run by wise and knowledgeable people. In order to prove his point, Galton collected all bets made at a fair about how much meat a bull would yield after being slaughtered. He then averaged them and compared them to the winning answer. Much to his dismay, he found that the average was closer to the reality than the most educated guess. He repeated the experiment several times and was always proven wrong in his intuition. Surowiecki's book goes on to provide a rich array of disturbing present-day examples.

13. J. Badaracco (1997) *Defining Moments: When managers must choose between right and right* (Harvard Business School Press).

Fons Trompenaars and Charles Hampden-Turner are amongst the key leaders in terms of cross-cultural issues. Their firm's website is http://www.thtconsulting.com/welcome/index.htm.

14. J. P. Sartre (1948/1972) *Les mains sales* (Gallimard).

3. BUILDING ECONOMIC VALUE THROUGH THE APPROPRIATE LEADERSHIP STYLE (THE BEHAVIORAL AGENDA)

1. See Billy Ray's 2007 film *Breach*, based on the true story of an FBI agent who decided to spy for the USSR because he felt undervalued. His superiors certainly never intended to produce such a result.

2. *A Bridge Too Far* (the 1977 film directed by Richard Attenborough) shows how British Military Intelligence, flatly ignoring the warnings of the Dutch resistance and building several unchecked assumptions into their plans, sent their soldiers to death in the battle of Arnhem.

The film was based on the journalist Cornelius Ryan's book of the same name. Ryan (1920–1974) was also author of *The Longest Day* (1959), which was also made into a highly successful movie.

3. The " Pygmalion effect," also called the "teacher expectancy effect," was the subject of intensive study by Robert Rosenthal (a German-born professor of psychology at the University of California in Riverside) and Lenore Jacobson (the principal of an elementary school in San Francisco). The results of their research were reported in their 1992 book *Pygmalion in the Classroom* (expanded edn, Irvington).
4. Paul Hersey leads the Center for Leadership Studies (http://www. situational.com/) and Ken Blanchard can be found on http://www.blanchard training.com/.
5. Margaret Wheatley is the President of the Berkana Institute, a charitable leadership foundation (http://www.berkana.org).
6. Margaret Wheatley and Myron Kellner-Rogers (1996) "The irresistible future of organizing," July/August, from Margaret Wheatley's website at http://www.berkana.org/, quoted with her permission.
7. The Hay Group's website is http://www.haygroup.com/.

4. UNLEASHING POTENTIAL THROUGH THE EMOTIONAL AGENDA

1. This book has been reprinted several times. The German edition can be found as *trotzdem ja zum Leben sagen: Ein Psychologe erlebt das Konzentrationslager*, by Viktor E. Frankl Kösel; Auflage: 8., Aufl. (2002); the English language edition is *Man's Search for Meaning* by Viktor E. Frankl, Beacon Press; 1st edition (2006).
2. See the helpful summary in *Time* magazine, 7 February 2007: "The new science of happiness."
3. *Les yeux dans les Bleus* (1998) directed by Stéphane Meunier. A documentary film that follows the 1998 French team that won football's World Cup (from Charles Biétry/service des Sports Canal+).
4. J. Kouzes and B. Posner (2007) *The Leadership Challenge*, 4th Edn (Jossey-Bass).
5. "We are living in an era where connectivity is becoming truly ubiquitous. ... The communications industry continues to change and the internet is at the center of this transformation. Today, the internet is Nokia's quest" (statement on www.nokia.com website, 1 October 2007).
6. "This is possible if you have Christ in your heart," posted on 4 October 2006 on www.WorldNetDaily.com.
7. S. Covey (1989) *The Seven Habits of Highly Effective People: Powerful lessons in personal change*, 1st edn (Free Press).
8. *Les yeux dans les Bleus*. See Note 3.
9. The Institut de Médecine Environnementale is hosted on http://www.iem-group.eu. Dr Jacques Fradin co-wrote an inspiring book on *The Neuronal Entreprise* (*L'entreprise neuronale* by Alan Fustec and Jacques Fradin, Editions d'organisation, 2001).

    Henri Laborit (1914–1995) was a biologist and philosopher who was particularly interested in human behavior. Humanity owes to him the discovery of the first neuroleptic drug, chlorpromazine. Through his work on the concept of "action inhibition," he demonstrated that rats that were prevented from escaping or fighting against a threat were likely to develop somatic diseases.

10. Dr Paul McLean is an American physician. His evolutionary theory of the "triune brain" was the first to treat the brain as being split into three main components: The R-complex (also called reptilian), the limbic and the neo-cortex.

   On emotional hijack, see D. Goleman (1997) *Emotional Intelligence: Why it can matter more than IQ* (Bantam).

11. The "Dreyfus case" is one of the most infamous in the history of the French judicial system. Dreyfus (1859–1935), a French army captain of Jewish origin, was accused of passing military intelligence to Austria and condemned in a deeply flawed process. His public degradation gave rise to shocking anti-Semitic demonstrations. After years of imprisonment he was found innocent, thanks in part to the spectacular and courageous stand of Emile Zola, who wrote a famous editorial ("J'accuse!") in support of him.

12. M. J. Apter (2007) *Reversal Theory: The Dynamics of Motivation, Emotion and Personality*, 2nd edn (Oxford: Oneworld Publications). Michael Apter is the founder of Apter International (http://www.apterinternational.com/).

   On reversal theory, see the Wikipedia article of 30 November 2008, http://en.wikipedia.org/wiki/Reversal_Theory.

5. ACCELERATING CHANGE: THE LEADERSHIP ENGAGEMENT PROCESS

1. The amazing effort on stage of Steve Balmer amply deserves a closer look. It can be seen on www.google.com under "dance monkeyboy"...

2. Elisabeth Kübler-Ross (1926–2004) was a Swiss psychiatrist. In her early career in hospitals, she was shocked by the way patients with fatal illnesses were informed of their condition and subsequently treated, and even more by the absence of a process to support the families and friends after the loss of their loved ones. She came up with the five-stage model described in the text. Her most famous book is *On Death and Dying* (Simon & Schuster/ Touchstone, 1969).

3. Zing technology was created by an Australian, John Findlay. It is a simple-to-use "leadership engagement tool": participants are divided into discussion groups of six to ten people, each sitting at a table equipped with a small keyboard on which they can type. The input from all the tables is immediately projected onto large screens. The process is anonymous, ensuring more honest feedback, and everybody can see what each table says in real time. All comments can then be rapidly summarized, clustered, or prioritized. Other companies have developed more or less similar technologies. Crystal interactive is one we use from time to time. Zing Technology's website is http://www.anyzing.com/. Their representative in Europe is Keymove, led by an amazingly rich personality, Nick McRoberts (http://www.keymove.fr/). Crystal Interactive is run by Chris Elmitt (www.crystal-interactive.co.uk).

4. *12 Angry Men* (1957) directed by Sydney Lumet and starring Henry Fonda.

5. The picture shown in Figure 5.2 was drawn by artist Richard Erickson for an MTI client. In the United States a great organization, Learning Roots, was

quoted in several Harvard Business Review articles (http://www.rootlearning.com) and in Denmark "A bigger picture" basically aims at the same purpose (www.biggerpicture.dk).

6. G. B. Shaw (1893) *Mrs Warren's Profession* (act II).

7. B. Alban and B. Bunker (2006) *The Handbook of Large Group Methods: Creating systemic change in organizations and communities* (Jossey-Bass).

8. L. Gratton (2007) *Hot Spots* (Financial Times Prentice Hall).

9. A. Damasio (1999) *The Feeling of What Happens: Body, emotion and the making of consciousness* (Heinemann).

10. *Cliffhanger* (1997), directed by Renny Harlin, starring Sylvester Stallone.

11. William Schutz (1925–2002) introduced in 1958 a theory of interpersonal relations, based on his work on nuclear submarines for the US Navy. The psychometric that came out of it, the FIRO-B (Fundamental Interpersonal Relations Orientation-Behavior™) was the world's most commonly used tool in English until it was superseded by the MBTI.

12. *Gandhi* (1982), directed by Richard Attenborough, starring Ben Kingsley.

13. A. de St Exupery (2000) *Citadelle*, 10th edn (Folio/Gallimard).

14. http://www.leadingthoughts.com/talent /denning.php.

15. P. Goodwin and T. Page (2008) *From Hippos to Gazelles: How leaders create leaders* (Kingsham Press) is a very readable book that provides a good range of tools for change management, using metaphors and stories.

16. A. Mehrabian and S. R. Ferris (1967) "Inference of attitudes from nonverbal communication," *Journal of Counseling Psychology*, Vol. 31, No. 3, pp. 248–52.

6. CONCLUSION: FROM MYTHICAL HEROES TO BUSINESS LEADERS

1. For further and more complete information about Joseph Campbell and his legacy, go on http://www.jcf.org, the website of the Joseph Campbell Foundation.

2. J. Campbell (2004) *The Hero with a Thousand Faces*, commemorative edition (Bollingen).

3. http://www.davidpearlgroup.com/.

4. *Cast Away* (2000), directed by Robert Zemeckis.

5. For further details of Saarinen's work, see his website at http://www.esasaarinen.com.

6. *Cellular* (2004), directed by David R. Ellis.

7. *Million Dollar Baby* (2005), directed by Clint Eastwood, winner of four Oscars.

8. *Walk the Line* (2006), directed by James Mangold.

9. *When We Were Kings* (1996), directed by Leon Gast.

10. *Batman Begins* (2005), directed by Christopher Nolan.

11. *Fierce Creatures* (1997), directed by Robert Young.

12. *Gladiator* (2000), directed by Ridley Scott.

TRIBUTE

Illustrations: Leonie Hunn 2008
(www.mfc-artconsult.com/leoniehunn@hotmail.com).

INDEX

reactive state, 66, 83
Toffler, Alvin, 3, 132 (notes)
Toyota, xxi, 11, 29, 67, 100, 131
    (notes), 135 (notes)
Trigano, Serge, 47
Trompenaars, Fons, 35, 136
    (notes)
Twelve Angry Men, 100

V
value building behaviours, 44, 46,
    47, 48, 99
  ask for time-out, 53
  ask open questions, 49, 50
  clarify, 53
  give feedback/run a review, 54
  listen actively, 48, 49
  summarize, 50
  support and constructively
    challenge, 51
value matrix, 9, 10, 14, 15, 16
  dream, 11
  heaven, 10, 16
  hell, 12, 14, 16

  nightmare, 10
Van Heck, Nick, 9, 30, 34
Varela, Francisco, 27, 31, 135
    (notes)
Verdin, Paul, 9

W
Walk the Line, 127, 139 (notes)
Wheatley, Margaret, 58, 135
    (notes), 137 (notes)
Wikinomics, 7, 133 (notes)
Wikipedia, 17, 18, 19, 21, 133
    (notes), 138 (notes)
Williams, Anthony D., 7, 133
    (notes)
Wilson, Barry, 47

Y
Youtube, 10, 119

Z
Zagalo, Mario, 76
Zing technology, 96, 101, 138
    (notes)